SHEET METAL WORKER MCQ

OBJECTIVE QUESTION ANSWERS

MANOJ DOLE

Made with ♥ on the Notion Press Platform
www.notionpress.com

Digitization is the need of the time. In the future, training in industrial training institutes will need to be conducted using online internet to make training more convenient and easy. E-books containing a set of MCQ questions will be made available to the trainees as they need to be more accustomed to the multiple choice questions MCQ to prepare for the online exams taking place in their industrial training institutes.

With all these factors in mind, Mr. Manoj Madhukar Dole Instructor, Industrial Training Institute, Satara, has written books according to the new annual system and NSQF-5 syllabus. And they've created theoretical mobile apps and blogs to make training easier, and made all these educational materials available for download on the world famous websites Google Play Store, Amazon and Apple Book Store.

The books were published by Hon'ble Joint Director Shri Rajendra Ghume Saheb Regional Office of Vocational Education and Training, Pune on 9/1/2019, at this time Shri Prakash Saigavkar Saheb Principal Government Industrial Training Institute Aundh Pune, Shri Tukaram Misal Saheb Principal Govt. Q. Sanstha Satara, Shri Sachin Dhumal Saheb District Vocational Education and Training Officer Satara, Shri Yatin Pargaonkar Saheb Principal Govt. Q. Sanstha Kolhapur, Shri Vikas Teke Saheb Inspector Vocational Education and Training Regional Office Pune, Palekar Foods Products Pvt. Ltd. Entrepreneurial Chairman of Satara Mr. Nilkanthrao Palekar Saheb, Chairman of Hira Foods Mr. Ibrahim Baba Tamboli Saheb, Mrs. Shalmali Pawar Headmaster Government Technical School Center Satara and other dignitaries were present on the occasion.

Contents

Prologue

Sheet Metal Worker MCQ is a simple Book for ITI & Engineering Course, Revised NSQ level Syllabus, It contains objective questions with underlined & bold correct answers MCQ covering all topics including all about the latest & Important about make, install and repair articles and parts of articles of sheet metal such as sheet steel, copper, tin, brass, aluminium, zinc or galvanized iron. Sheet Metal Worker, makes sheet metal articles according to drawing or sample. Studies drawing or sample and records measurements if necessary. Selects sheet of required type, thickness (gauge) and size and marks it with scriber, square, divider, foot rule etc., according to drawing or sample. Shears wherever necessary by machine or hand shears and makes it to required shape and size by bending, seaming, forming, riveting, soldering etc., using mallets, hammers, formers, sets, stakes, etc., or by various machines such as shearing, bending, beading, channeling , circle cutting. Checks work at stages during operations and does soldering, brazing, arc welding, gas welding, TIG welding & MIG welding as necessary. May undertake aluminum paneling work. May also undertake repair work. May specialize indifferent metal sheets such as tin, copper, brass

We add new question answers with each new version. Please email us in case of any errors/omissions. This is arguably the largest and best e-Book for All engineering multiple choice questions and answers.

As a student you can use it for your exam prep. This e-Book is also useful for professors to refresh material.

Foreword

Vocational education and training is imparted through the Department of Vocational Education and Training through the Department of Business Education and Business Practical to supply multi-skilled artisans in line with the rapidly growing demand in the industrial sector in the 21st century. All the occupations within the institutions are important, as the trainees from these occupations develop multi-skills as per the demands of the industry.

with the noble intention of making available MCQ e-books suitable for all businesses, considering that all the examinations in all the industries in the industrial sector are conducted online and include MCQ method questions. Mr. Manoj Madhukar Dole has written a very good e-book on MCQ method as per the new annual syllabus. This e-book will definitely be a guide for all the trainees, trainee candidates, training instructors and others concerned.

The author of the book is Mr. Manoj Madhukar Dole, Instructor Gov. ITI Satara has 17 years of training experience. Written as a new annual pattern, this e-book incorporates modern digital QR Code technology to understand the layout, simple language, and simple syntax, diagrams and videos for each subject. So I am sure that this e-book will definitely be useful for in-depth study and exam practice. The work they have done is certainly commendable.

Mr. Tukaram Misal
Principal Government Industrial Training Institute Satara.

Preface

DGET New Delhi and CSTARI Kolkata have been implementing an annual pattern for all businesses in ITI since the August 2018 session. The examination system will also be changed and it will be online from this year and since all the questions are of Objective Type (MCQ), the trainees are in dire need of in-depth study. It is with this in mind that we are delighted to present the books based on the old NIMI pattern and a complete overview of the new annual pattern, and we hope that these books will be a guide for all business directors and trainees. Is.

For writing these books, Johar Awate Saheb, Principal of ITI Akluj. Former Principal of ITI Satara Saigavkar Saheb, Assistant Director Shri Chandrakant Dhekne Saheb Regional Office of Vocational Education and Training, Pune, District Vocational Education and Training Officer Sachin Dhumal Saheb and Headmaster Government Technical School Kendra Shalmali Pawar Madam and son Adhiraj Dole, mother Kusum Dole, I am very grateful to my father Madhukar Dole and wife Ashwini Dole for their special guidance and cooperation from time to time.

Also, in a very short period of time, the book was reviewed by Shri Rajendra Ghume Saheb, Joint Director, Vocational Education and Training Regional Office, Pune, for his invaluable time in publishing the book. I am sincerely grateful for their feedback.

I am grateful to the Instructor of ITI Satara for there continuous support from the very beginning of writing the book.

From this book, I consider myself blessed to have shared my thoughts on e-learning with you. I will not claim that this book is perfect, because considering the perfection, this book is an attempt and is in its infancy. They will be valuable for improvement if they are tested and suggested.

Manoj Dole
Dated 9/1/2019

Acknowledgements

The industrial training and theoretical examination system of our industrial training institutes and these changes have been accepted by the craft instructors and the trainees. Theoretical examinations conducted in your industrial training institutes are also conducted online. Since these examinations are of multiple choice MCQ method, the trainees will need to get more practice of such questions.

With all these considerations in mind, Mr. Manoj Madhukar, Director, Dole Crafts, Katari Industrial Training Institute, Satara, has done a thorough study and with his diligent work and added his keen intellect, according to the new annual system and NSQF-5 syllabus, e-book of Katari and other machine trades. -Book) and they have created mobile apps and blogs on theoretical topics to make training easier and have made all these educational materials available for download on the world famous websites Google Play Store, Amazon and Apple Book Store. Training has been made easier by creating a print version and using advanced techniques like QR Code.

All these educational materials will definitely be a guide for all the trainees for in-depth study and for the craft instructors and other concerned who are imparting vocational training.

CHAPTER ONE

Sheet Metal Worker MCQ Drawing

Online Test Exam | ITI Books | CNC Course | AutoCAD CAM | JOB & Apprentice

Online Theory | Computer Course | Trading Course | Web Designing | MSCIT Course

Shopping Business | Internet Business | Remotasks Course | Online Services | Top Sportsmans

Indian Army | Freedom Fighters | Top Scientists | Social Reformers | Motivational Speaker

Top Richest People | Join WhatsApp Group | Join Facebook Group | Like Facebook Page | PAN / Adhar / Licence Passport

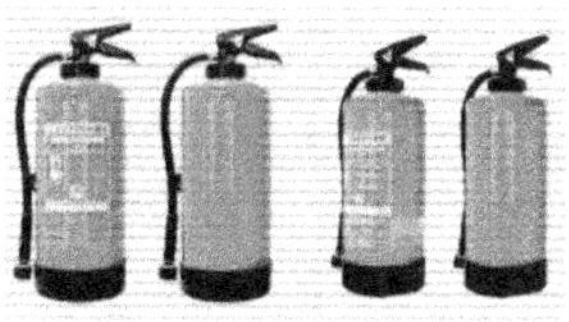

Fire extinguisher

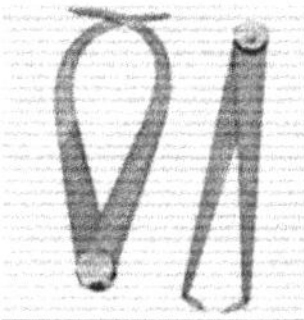

Calliper

Hacksaw frame

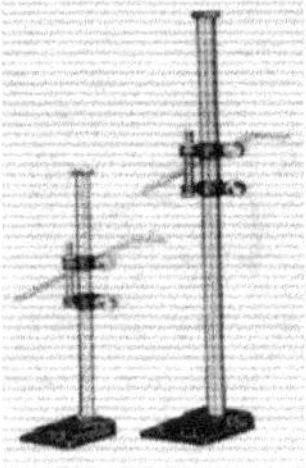

Universal surface guage

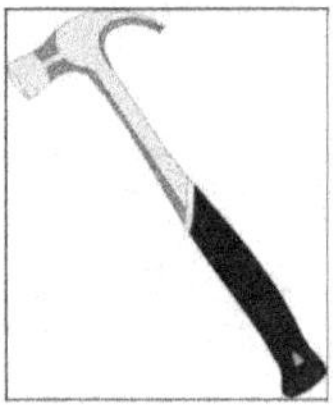

Hammer

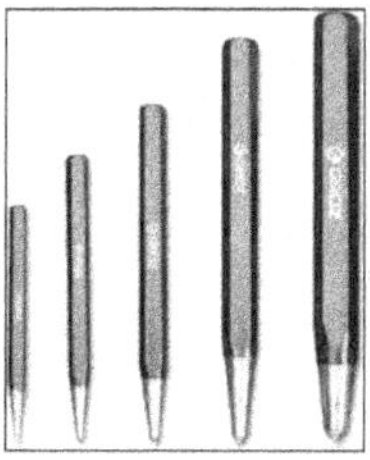

Centre punch

Bench vice

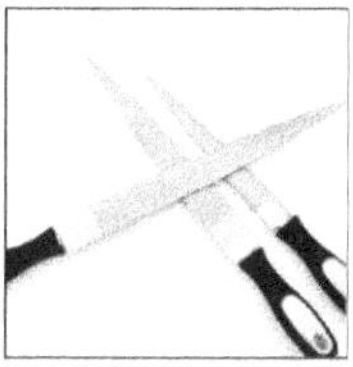

Files

Scraper

Surface Plate

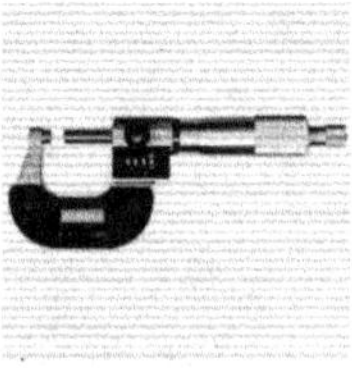

Outside Micrometer

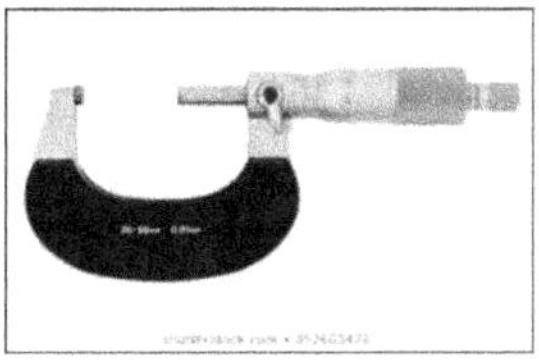

Micrometer

Depth micrometer

Vernier Calliper

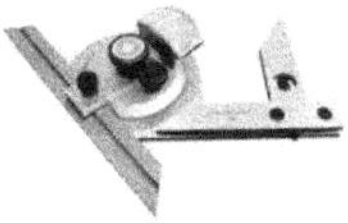

Vernier bevel protractor

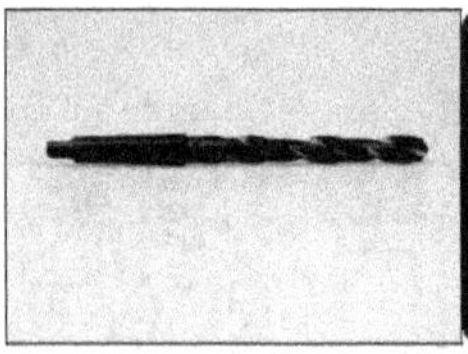

Drilling

Reamer

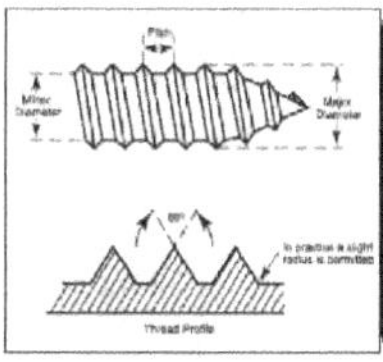

Thread

Tap Die

Grinding Wheel

Tap Die

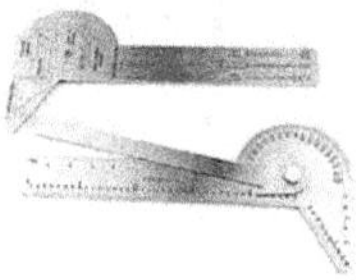

Centre gauge

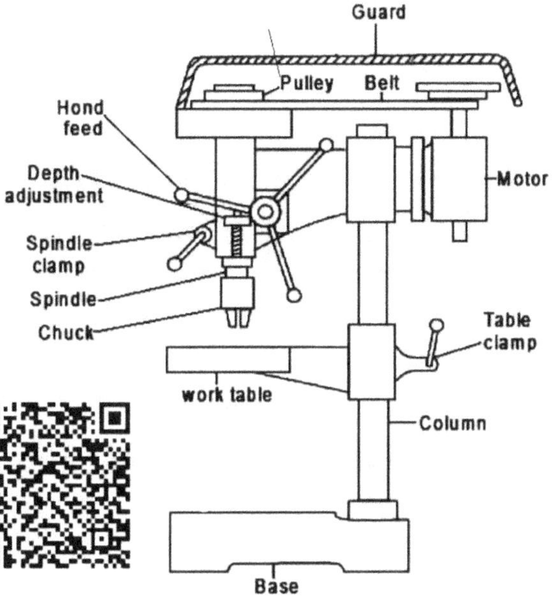

Piller Drilling Machine

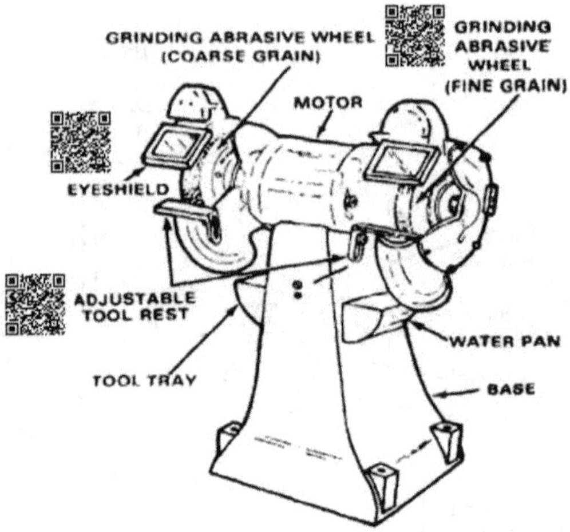

Pedastal Grinding Machine

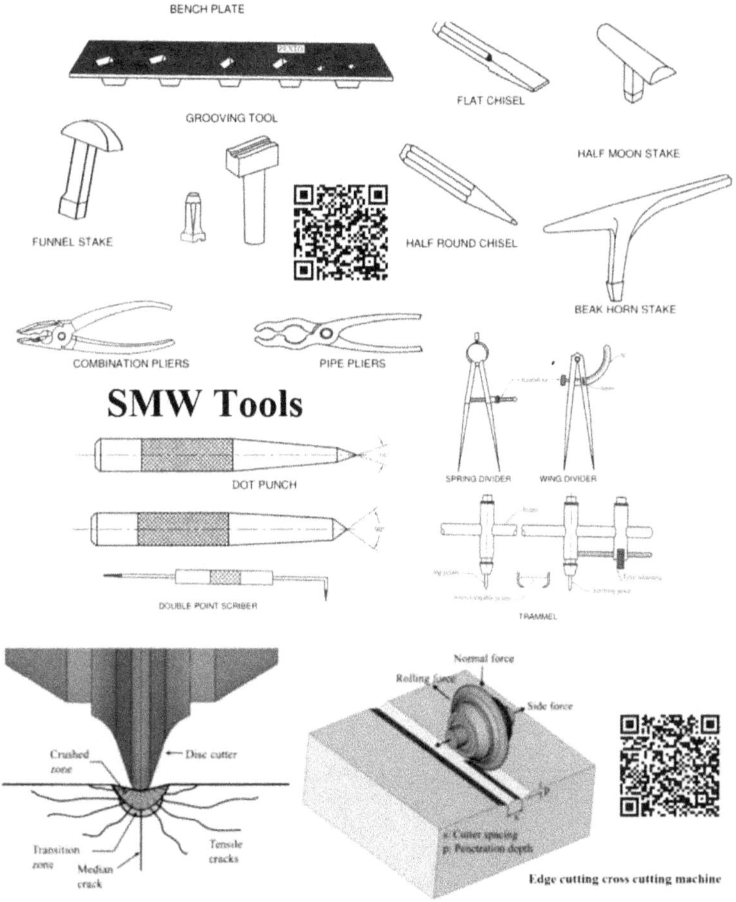
BENCH PLATE
FLAT CHISEL
GROOVING TOOL
HALF MOON STAKE
FUNNEL STAKE
HALF ROUND CHISEL
BEAK HORN STAKE
COMBINATION PLIERS
PIPE PLIERS
SMW Tools
SPRING DIVIDER
WING DIVIDER
DOT PUNCH
DOUBLE POINT SCRIBER
TRAMMEL
Crushed zone
Disc cutter
Transition zone
Median crack
Tensile cracks
Normal force
Rolling force
Side force
s: Cutter spacing
p: Penetration depth
Edge cutting cross cutting machine

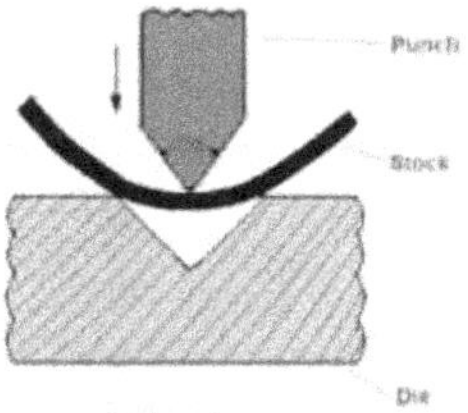

V-Bending

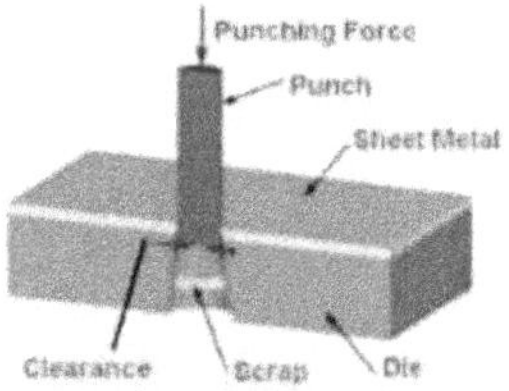

Punching Operation

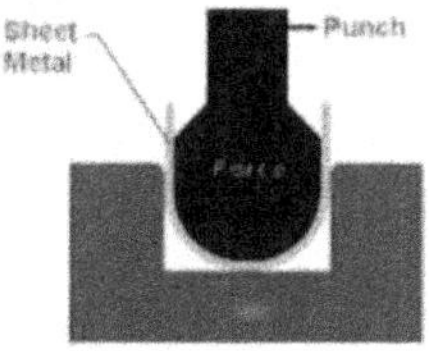

U-Bending

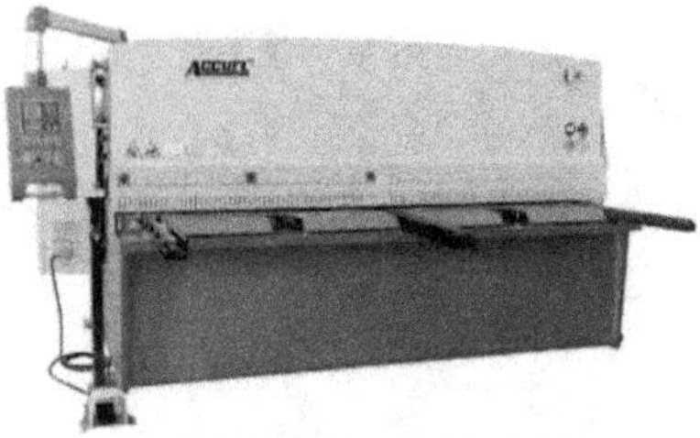

Hydraulic Shearing Machine

Rotary Shearing Machine

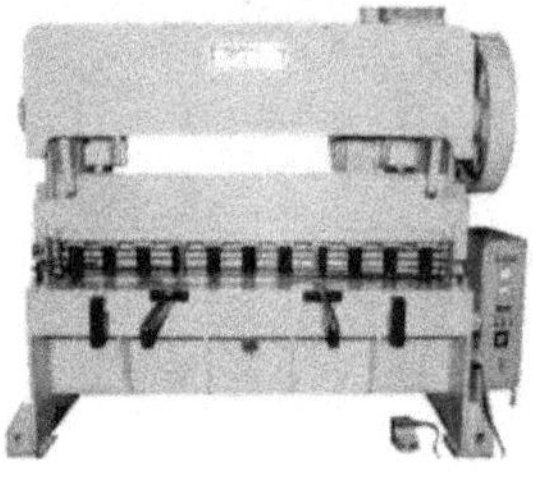

Pneumatic Shearing Machine

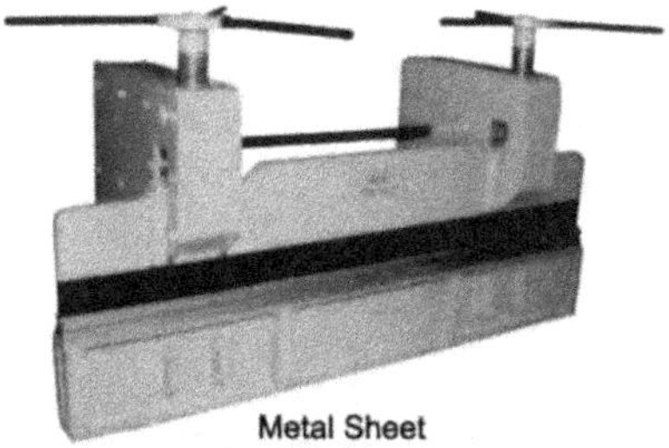

Metal Sheet
Bending Machine

Pipe Bending Machine

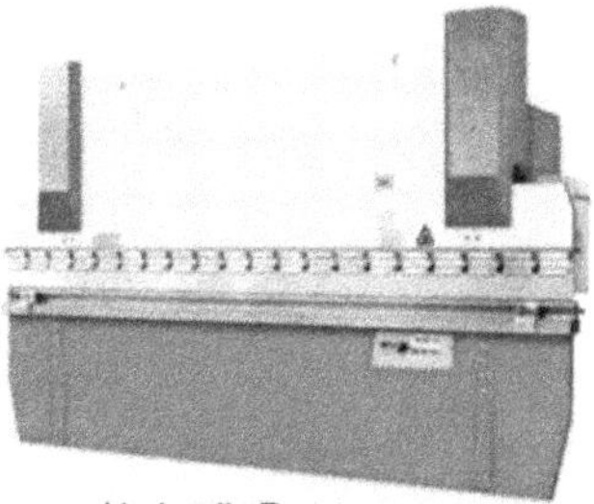

Hydraulic Press
Brake Machine

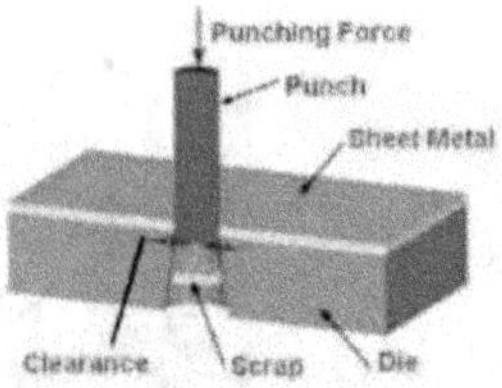

Punching Operation

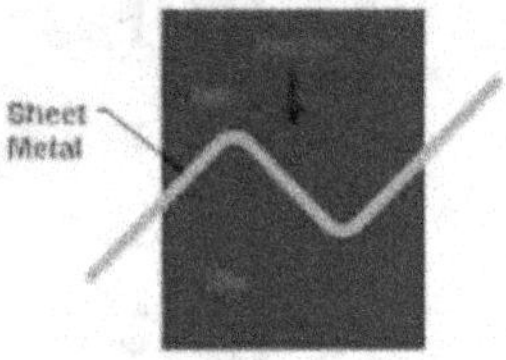

Offset Bending

Channel Bending

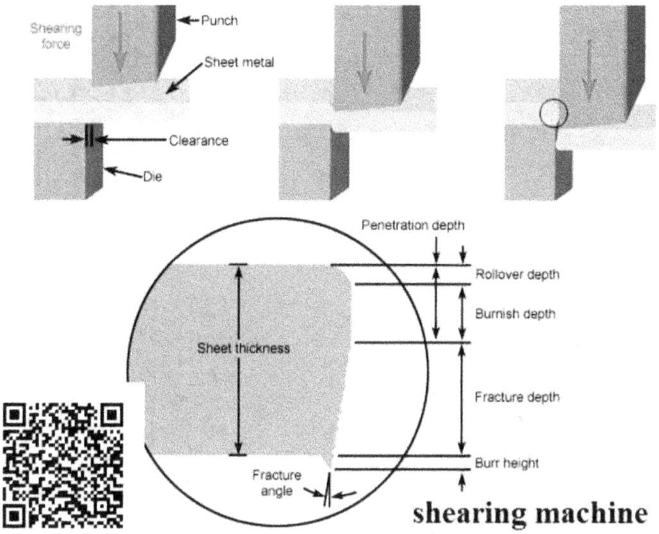
Shearing force
Punch
Sheet metal
Clearance
Die
Penetration depth
Rollover depth
Burnish depth
Sheet thickness
Fracture depth
Burr height
Fracture angle
shearing machine

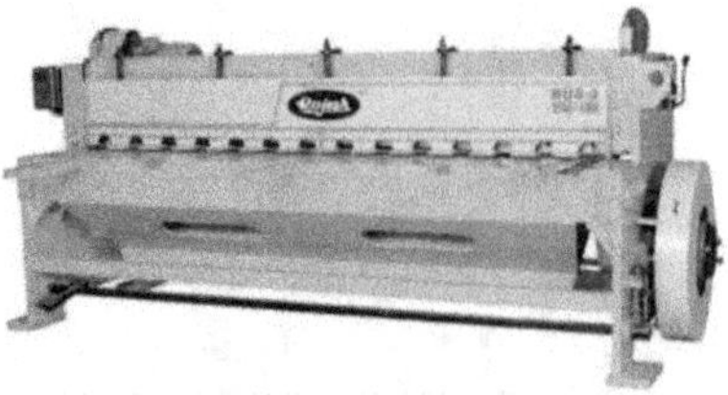

Mechanical Shearing Machine

Alligator Shearing Machine

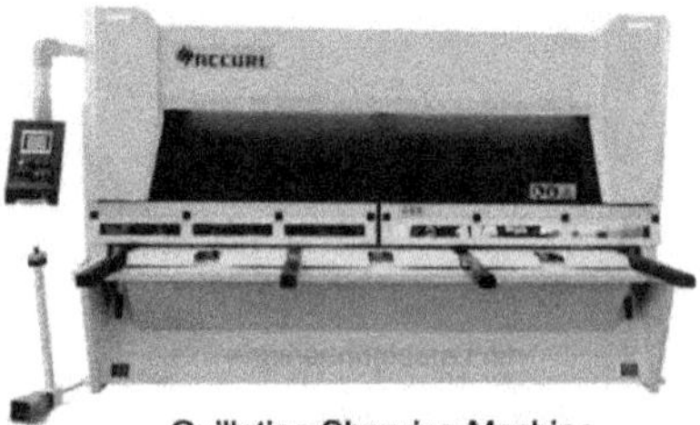

Guillotine Shearing Machine

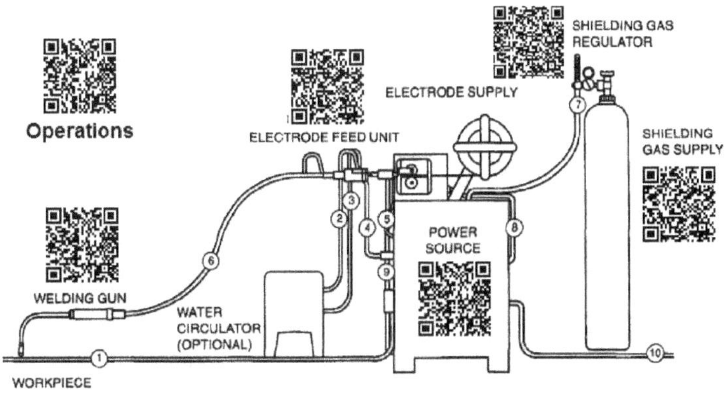

Gas Metal Arc Welding

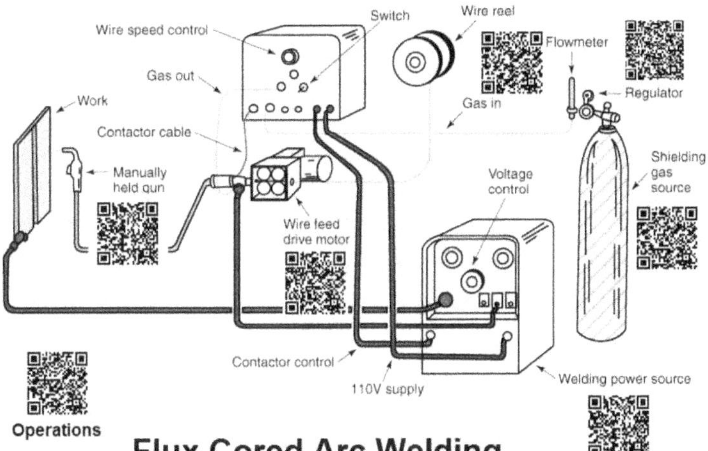

Flux Cored Arc Welding

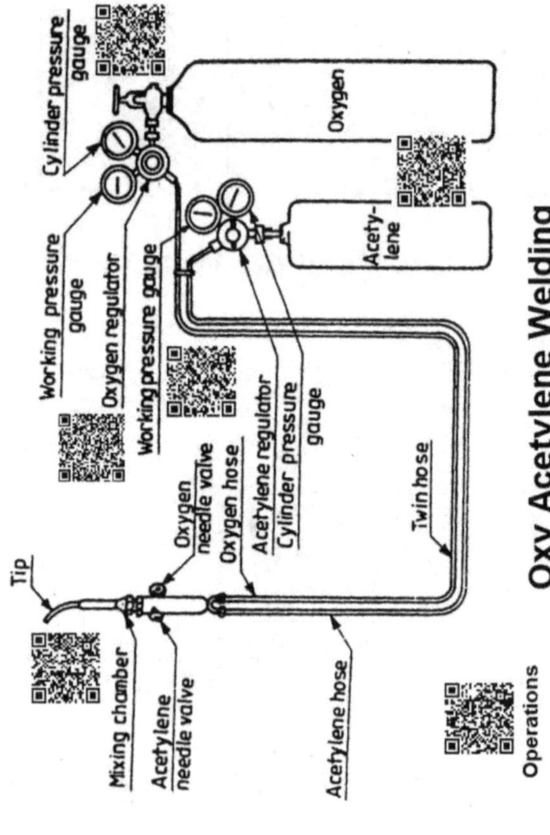

Oxy Acetylene Welding

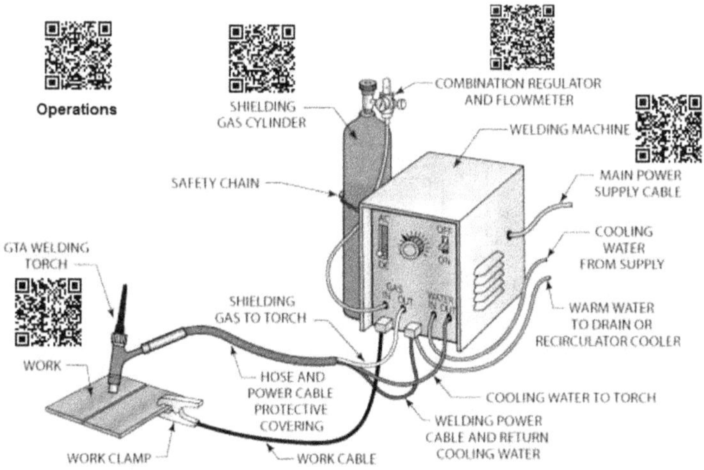

GTAW EQUIPMENT

(GAS TUNGSTEN ARC WELDING)

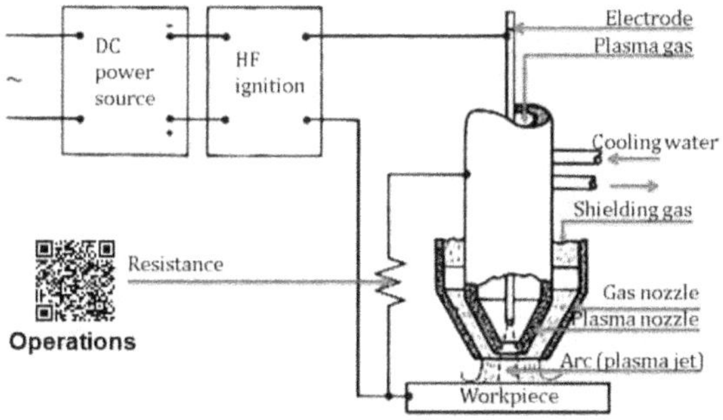

Plasma Transferred Arc Welding

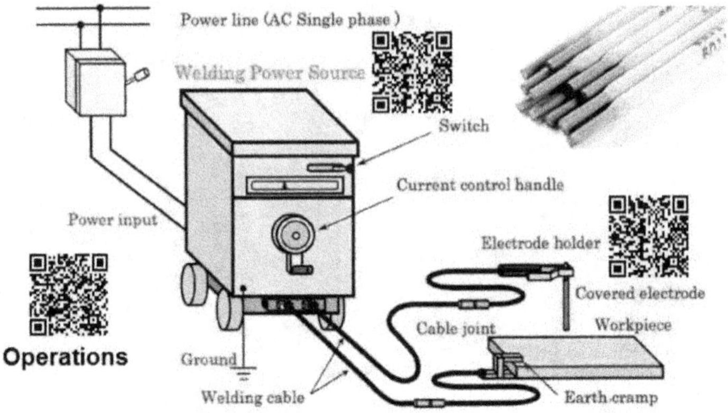

Shielded Metal Arc Welding

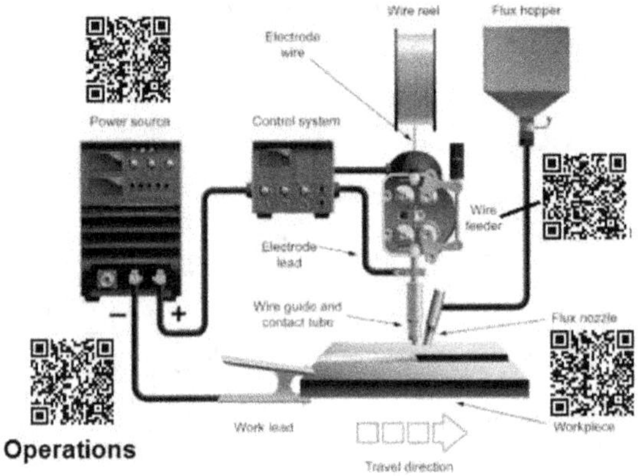

Submerged Arc Welding

CHAPTER TWO

Sheet Metal Worker MCQ

1] Which one is a workshop safety?

A] Keep shop floor clean and free from grease, oil or other slippery materials

B] Stop the machine before changing the speed

C] Don't use cracked or chipped tools

D] Don't try to stop a running machine with hand

2] In Personal Protect Equipment (PPE] HELMET is used to

A] protect head

B] Protect eyes

C] Protect hands

D] Protect ears

3] Which of the following belongs to general safety?

A Have a worker in good attitude

B] The work clean and clear

C] Concentrate on your work

D] Keep the floor and gangways clean and clear

4] While grinding, which is used to protect the eyes?

A] Dark green glass

B] Mask

C] Sun glasses

D] Safety goggles

5] Which of the following is done for machine safety?

A] Check the oil level before starting the machine

B] Do things in a methodical way

C] Keep the floor and gangways clean and clear

D] Don't use dies and scarves

6] In Personal Protect Equipment (PPE], 'sleeves' is used to protect ----------

A] Face
B] Eyes
C] Ears
D] Hands
7] ABC stands for --------------
A] Automatic Breathing Control
B] Automatic Blood Control
C] Airway Breathing Circulation
D] Automatic Blood Circulation
8] Fire & FIRE EXTINGUISHERS

Fire extinguisher

9] To put off"Class B" fire, the types of fire extinguisher used is ....
A] dry power
B] Carbon dioxide
C] Jet of water
D] Foam type
10] Which type of fire extinguisher is used to put off general fire?
A] Water type Extinguisher
B] Foam type Extinguisher
C] Dry chemical powder Extinguisher
D] Carbon dioxide (C02] Extinguisher
11] In case of bleeding, take treatment Of
D] cold 3" and rest
A] spray cold water
B] Bandage immediately -----.
B] Enquire about the accident thought treatment

12] in case of an accident, the victim should im

A] Asked to take rest

<u>C] Attended immediately</u>

D] leave him

13] First aid is given to an injured or ill person primarily....

A] Save life

B] Prevent further deterioration of the muff's

C] Give best possible comfort

<u>D] All of these</u>

14] Colour code for Bins for waste paper segregation is -----

<u>A] blue Colour</u>

B] Yellow Colour

C] Red Colour

D] Green Colour

15] In Japanese Seiko stands for --------------

<u>A] Shine</u>

B] Sort

C] Standardize

D] Sustain

16] Benefit of SS system is ------

A] Increase in productivity

B] Increase in quality

C] Reduction in wastage of time

<u>D] All of these</u>

17] Safety is -----------

A] nobody's business

<u>B] every bodise business</u>

C] Some bodies business

D] The organization business

18] For basic categories of safety signs are available The meaning of"prohibition" sign ----

A] shows it must not be done

B] Shows what must be done

C] Warns the hazard or danger

D] Gives information of safety provision

18] One micrometer (U] is equal to...

A] 0.1mm

B] 0.01mm

C] 0.001mm

D] 0.0001mm

19] The caliper meant for measuring the width of a slot is...

A] Odd leg caliper

B] Outside caliper

C] Jenny caliper

D] Inside calliper

Calliper

20] The size of the dividers are specified by the -----------

A] Total length of legs

B] Distance between the points when fully opened

C] Length of legs without points

D] distance between the pivot and the point

21] The instrument used to mark parallel lines, parallel to the datum edge is -

A] jenny caliper

B] Divider

C] Outside calliper

D] Inside calliper

22] Which one of the following is an indirect measuring tool?

A] Outside caliper

B] Vernier calliper

C] Steel rule

D] Outside micrometer

23] For cutting thin tubing, the most suitable pitch of the hacksaw blade is...

A] 1.8mm

B] 1.4mm

C] 1mm

D] 0.8mm

24] For cutting solid brass, the most suitable pitch of the hacksaw blade is...

A] 1.8mm

B] 1.4mm

C] 1mm

D] 0.8mm

Hacksaw frame

25] A new hacksaw blade after a few strokes becomes loose because of the...

A] Stretching of the blade

B] Wing-nut threads being worn out

C] Wrong pitch of the blade

D] Improper selection of the set of saws.

26] While cutting small diameter pipes, it is advisable to watch regularly and ensure that...

A] The cut is along the curved line

B] More saw teeth are in contract

C] The work is not overheated

D] Proper balancing of hacksaw is maintained

27] The vice clamps are used to...

A] Protect hard jaws

B] Clamp the work pieces rigidly

C] Protect the finished surfaces

D] Prevent the movable jaw being filed

28] The reference surface during marking is provided by the...

A] Surface gauge

B] Workpiece

C] Drawing of the work

D] Marking table surface

29] The size of an engineer's vice is specified by the...

A] Length of the movable jaw

B] Width of the jaws

C] Height of the vice

D] Maximum opening of the jaws

30] The part of the universal surface gauge which helps to draw a parallel line along a datum edge is the..

A] Rocker arm

B] Snug

C] Fine adjustment screw

D] Guide pins

Universal surface guage

31] Scribers are made of...

A] Mild steel

B] High carbon steel

C] Brass

D] Cast iron

32] Portion of the hammer used for fixing the handle is...

A] Face

B] Peen
C] Cheek
D] Eye hole

33] Weight of the hammer for the marking purpose is...
A] 250g
B] 500g
C] 1 kg
D] 2 kgs

Hammer

34] The size of the dividers are specified by the...
A] Total length of the legs
B] Distance between the points when fully opened
C] Length of legs without the points
D] Distance between the pivot and the point

35] The included angle of the groove of 'V' block is always....
A] 45°
B] 60°
C] 90°
D] 120°

36] 'V' blocks are available in grades of...
A] A & B
B] A,B & C
C] 1,2 & 3
D] 1 & 2

37] 'V' blocks of grade 'B' are made of
A] Cast iron
B] Mild steel
C] Steel

D] Cast steel

38] Name the punch used to locate the centre.

A] Prick punch 30°

B] Prick punch 60°

C] Centre punch

D] Dot punch

Centre punch

39] The point angle of centre punch is --------

A] 30°

B] 50°

c] 900

D] 1200

40] Punches are used for forming ---------of any shape

A] Holes

B] Mining

C] Knurling

D] Reaming

41] Generally the length of the handle of the vice is ----------

A] 1.5 times the normal size of the vice

B] 2.5 times the normal size of the vice

C] 3.5 times the normal size of the vice

D] 4.5 times the normal size of the vice

Bench vice

42] Bench vice spindle is made of ....

A] mild steel

B] Cast iron

C] Tool steel

D] Bronze

43] The convexity of files helps...

A] To file concave surfaces

B] To file convex surfaces

C] To prevent rounding of edges of work

D] The file to become straight when pressure is applied

Files

44] Which file used for filling wood, leather and other soft material? .

A] Single cut file

B] Double cut file

c] Rasp cut file

D] Curved cut file

45] File used is used for ------------

A] Cleaning the work piece

C] Renewing the file teeth

B] cleaning the file teeth

D] Cleaning the chips

46] File card is used to --------

A] Clean the work piece

C] Renew the file teeth

B] Clean the file teeth

47] The point angle of scriber is -----------

A] 30°

B] 60°

C] 5° to 10°

D] 12° to 15°

48] The cutting angle for chipping cast iron is...

A] 37.5°

B] 55°

C] 60°

D] 90°

49] The chisel will dig into the material when...

A] The rake angle is more

B] The clearance angle is too low

C] The angle of inclination is more

D] The angle of inclination is too low

50] A slight convexity is given to the cutting edge to...

A] Cut curved surfaces

B] Cut sharp corners

C] Prevent digging of the ends

D] Allow the lubricant to enter

51] Surface plates are made of...

A] High grade cast steel

B] Fine-grained cast iron

C] Alloy steels

D] Wrought iron

52] Surface plates are specified by their length and breadth & are in
A] decimetre
B] Cubic meter
C] Cylindrical
53] Ribs are given on the unmachined portion of the angle plate for...
A] Easy handling
B] Convenience in manufacturing
C] Clamping while setting on machines
D] Rigidity and to prevent distortion
54] The slots on the angle plate are given for...
A] Reducing weight
B] Aligning the work
C] Lifting using hooks
D] Accommodating bolts.
55] The size of the angle plates is stated by...
A] Weight
B] Length
C] Length x width
D] Size number
56] for high speed parting off work on material like cemented carbide Is'
A] Do all machine
B] Cutting off machine
C] Heavy duty power saw
D] Mining machine sitting saw
57] Gun metal is an alloy of copper, ------------
A] tin and zinc
B] Lead and zinc
C] Zinc and nickel
D] Lead and nickel
58] Cast iron is used for manufacturing machine beds because -------

A] it can resist more compressive stress
B] it is heavy in weight
C] It is cheaper metal
D] It is a brittle metal
59] Accuracy or least count of a metric outside micrometric is ---------
A] 0-1 mm
B] 0.01 mm
C] 0.001 mm
D] 0.02 mm

60] 1000 microns means -----
A] 1 mm
B] 1 m
C] 1000 mm
D] 10 cm
61] in a metric micrometer, a complete revolution of thimble advances -----------
A] 0.01 mm
B] 0.25 mm
C] 0.50 mm
D] 1.00mm

Micrometer

62] Ratchet Stop in the micrometer helps to ------------

A] Control the pressure

B] lock the spindle

C] Adjust the zero error

D] Hold the work piece

63] 1000 micron means ------------

A] 1 mm

B] 1 m

C] 1000 mm

D] 10 cm

64] What is the zero reading of a 50-75 mm outside micrometer?

A] 0.000 mm

B] 0.01 mm

C] 25.00 mm

D] 50.00 mm

65] The value of the smallest division on sleeve of a metric outside micrometer is -----

A] 0.50 mm

B] 1.00 mm

C] 1.50 mm

D] 2.00 mm

66] Ratchet stop in the micrometer helps to ---------

A] control the pressure

B] Lock the spindle

C] Adjust the zero error

D] Hold the work piece

67] Least count of depth micrometer is

A] 0.5 mm

B] 0.2 mm

C] 0.001 mm

D] 0.01 mm

Depth micrometer

68] The least count of vernier calliper is (main scale = 49 division, vernier scale = 50 division]

A] 0.1 mm

B] 0.01 mm

C] 0.001 mm

D] 0.02 mm

Vernier Calliper

69] The type of measurement made by using a Vernier Calliper is -------

A] Direct measurement

B] Indirect measurement

C] 90“] (a] 81 (b]

D] None of these

70] The least count of a vernier bevel protractor is...

A] 1”

B] 5’

C] 1◦

D] 5 ◦

71] The part of a vernier bevel protractor which is normally used as a reference base for measuring angles is the...

A] Blade

B] Stock

C] Disc

C] Main scale

Vernier bevel protractor

72] The part of a vernier bevel protector on which main scale divisions are marked is the...

A] Stock

B] Dial

C] Disc

D] Adjustable blade

73] The part of a bevel protractor, which comes in contact with the inclined surface while measuring is the...

A] Blade

B] Stock

C] Disc

D] Dial

74] The value of each division of the main scale of a vernier bevel protractor is...

A] 5'

B] 1°

C] 5°

D]10°

75] The value of each division of the vernier scale of a bevel protractor is...

A] 1°

B] 1◦5'

C] 1◦55'

D] 5'

76] The taper shank drills are held on the machine by means of...

A] Chucks

B] Sleeves

C] Drift

D] Vice

77] Drill chucks are fitted on the drilling machine spindle by means of a...

A] Knurled ring

B] Arbor

C] Drift

D] Pinion and key

78] The Morse taper provided on drills ranges between...

A] MT 1 to MT 5

B] MT 1 to MT 4

C] MT 0 to MT 5

D] MT 0 to MT 4

79] A drift is used for...

A] Drawing a drill location

B] Fixing chuck on the machine spindle

C] Removing a broken drill from the work

D] Removing the drill from the machine spindle

80] When the taper shank of the drill is larger than the machine spindle, the device to hold the drill is a...

A] Drill sleeve

B] Taper socket

C] Drill drift

D] Chuck and key

81] The suitable cutting fluid for drilling mild steel in a drilling machine is...

A] Synthetic soluble oil
B] Neat oil
C] Distilled water
D] Soluble oil
82] A special feature of the radial drilling machine is...
A] It can be used for drilling with a H.S.S. drill
B] Table can be moved and set at any position
C] A variety of speeds is available
D] The spindle can be brought to any position

83] The point angle of drills depends on...
A] The size of the drill
B] The type of machine
C] The material of the work
D] The RPM of the drill
84] The point angle for a standard drill is...
A] 60°
B] 108°
C] 118°
D] 135°
85] The helical angle determines the...
A] Cutting angle
B] Chew angle
C] Rake angle
D] Lip angle
86] The clearance angle of the drill is between...
A] 3° to 5°
B] 8° to 12°

C] 12◦ to 20◦

D] 15◦ to 20◦

87] In a remote place (no electricity available] a rail track is to be drilled. Choose the right drilling machine

A] Radial drilling machine

B] Pillar drilling machine

C] Ratchet drilling machine

D] Sensitive drilling Machine

Drilling

88] A drilling machine used by a carpenter for cabinet making is a...

A] Ratchet drilling machine

B] Radial drilling machine

C] Breast drilling machine

D] Sensitive drilling machine

89] Which one of the following drilling machines is used for drilling holes where electricity is not available?

A] Bench drilling machine

B] Pillar drilling machine

C] Redial drilling machine

D] Ratchet drilling machine

90] Which one of the following drilling machine is used for heavy duty work?

A] Bench drilling machine

B] Pillar drilling machine

C] Radial drilling machine

D] Electric hand drilling machine

91] Drill chuck are held on the machine spindle by means of ------

A] arbor

B] Drift

C] draw-in bar

D] Chuck nut

92] Different speeds are obtained in a sensitive bench drilling machine by ----

A] Belt pulley mechanism

B] Hydraulic mechanism

C] Rack and Pinion mechanism

D] Cam and follower mechanism

103] Gun metal is an alloy of copper, ------------

A] tin and zinc

B] Lead and zinc

C] Zinc and nickel

D] Lead and nickel

104] for making gutters, roof flashing, hoods etc.

A] Galvanised iron

B] Stainless steel

C] Copper sheet

D] Metal sheets

105] in dairies. food processing, kitchen ware etc.

A] Galvanised iron

B] Stainless steel

C] Copper sheet

D] Metal sheets

106] for making buckets, heating ducts, cabinets etc.

A] Galvanised iron

B] Stainless steel

C] Copper sheet

D] Metal sheets

107] Punching a number of holes in a sheet is known as?

a) Perforating

b) Parting

c) Notching

d) Lancing

108] Shearing the sheet into two or more pieces is known as?

a) Perforating

b) Parting

c) Notching

d) Lancing

109] Removing the pieces from the edge in shearing operation is known as?

a) Perforating
b) Parting
c) Notching
d) Lancing

110] Leaving a tab without removing any material is known as?

a) Perforating
b) Parting
c) Notching
d) Lancing

111] Moving a small straight punch up and down rapidly into a die is done by a process known as?

a) Perforating
b) Parting
c) Nibbling
d) Lancing

112] As the thickness of sheet is increased the clearance needed will also?

a) Increase
b) Decrease
c) No effect
d) First decrease then increase

113] Bevelling is particularly suitable for shearing of?

a) Thin blanks
b) Thick blanks
c) Very thin blanks
d) None of the Mentioned

114] Which of the following is a type of die?

a) Simple dies
b) Progressive dies
c) Compound die
d) All of the Mentioned

115] Which of the following die can perform multiple operations such as blanking, punching, notching etc.?

a) Simple dies
b) Progressive dies
c) Compound die

d) None of the Mentioned

182] Which one of the following is used only for finishing and maintaining correct form of thread?

A] Tap

B] Threading tool

C] Threading chaser

D] Tipped tool

188] A die in which more than one cutting operation is per formed in one stroke

A] Piercing die

B] Progressive die

C] Combination die

D] Compound die

189] A die in which cutting and non cutting operations are carried out per stroke.

A] Piercing die

B] Progressive die

C] Combination die

D] Compound die

Tap Die

190] A die in which two or more sequential operations are performed at two or more stations upon the work.

A] Piercing die

B] Progressive die

C] Combination die

D] Compound die

191] A die in which the shape of the punch and die are directly reproduced in the metal with little or no metal flow.

A] Progressive die

B] Combination die

C] Compound die

D] Forming die

192] The die used for producing any shape of holes.

A] Piercing die

B] Progressive die

C] Combination die

D] Compound die

193] Abrasives are classifications into.............

A] Two types

B] Three types

c] One types

D] Four types

194] Grinding wheels made out of---------------- abrasive are most common because of its free and cool cutting action.

A] Aluminium oxide

B] Silicon oxide

C] Ammonium oxide

D] Carbide.

195] Which among the following abrasive is mostly used for cutting off wheels for cutting non metallic materials?

A] Aluminium oxide

B] Silicon carbide

C] Diamond

D] None of above

196] Which abrasive particle is used for grinding tungsten carbide tool insert?

A] Silicon carbide

B] A|203

C] Diamond

D] Corundum

197] Which of the following is the natural abrasive?

A] Aluminium oxide

B] Silicon

C] Boron carbide

D] Corundum

198] Which of the following is the manufactured abrasive?

A] Corundum.

B] Quartz

C] Silicon

D] Emery

199] Which abrasive particle is used for grinding steel fittings?

A] Silicon carbide

B] Aluminium oxide

C] Diamond.

D] boron oxide

200] What kind of abrasive cut of wheel should be used to cut concrete stone and masonry?

A] Silicon

B] Al203

C] Diamond grit

D] Glass

201] Aluminium oxide wheel is used for grinding ------------

A] cast iron

B] Cemented carbide.

C] HSS ‘

D] ceramic

202] The bond of diamond wheel suitable for offhand grinding of the tipped tool is ....

A] Resinoid

B] Vitrified

C] Shellac

D] Metal

Grinding Wheel

318] The number of threads per inch can be checked with a

A] tool gauge

B] metric rule by counting

C] ring gauge

D] screw pitch gauge

screw pitch gauge

319] When threading, the carriage is moved along the ways by

A] a gear train on a track

B] the feed rod spline or key-way

C] the lead screw thred

D] the hand wheel

320] Thread chasers are used for

A] quick production of threads

B] maintaining an exact form of thread

C] cutting threads on hard materials

D] cutting threads on soft materials

Q 1. Which of the following is not a cause of accident

A). Awareness of danger

B). Disregard for safety

C). Lack of understanding of proper safety procedures

D). Improper use of tools

Q 2. What is the first action, if your friend receives a heavy electric shock

A). Pull the friend from the live conductor

B). Pour water to avoid burning of friend

C). Fetch the first aid box

D). Switch off the current immediately

Q 3. Match the following - Safety Signs Shape

(i) Prohibition Sign (p) Triangular

(ii) Warning Sign (q) Square

(iii) Information (r) Data

A). (i) - (r) ; (ii) - (p) ; (iii) - (q)
B). (i) - (p) ; (ii) - (r) ; (iii) - (q)
C). (i) - (r) ; (ii) - (q) ; (iii) - (p)
D). (i) - (q) ; (ii) - (p) ; (iii) - (r)

Q 4. Identify the Warning Sign as shown in figure -
A). Risk of Explosion
B). Risk of Electric Shock
C). Risk of ionizing Radiation
D). Risk of Fire

Q 5. The process of turning an edge on a circular piece of metal is called
A). Burring
B). Beading
C). Forming
D). Planishing

Q 6. Match the following - Types of Joint Allowance
(i) Grooved Joint (G) (p) 2W+3T
(ii) Panedown Joint (P) (q) 2W+2T
(iii) Knocked up Joint (K) (r) W
A). (i) - (r) ; (ii) - (p) ; (iii) - (q)
B). (i) - (p) ; (ii) - (r) ; (iii) - (q)
C). (i) - (r) ; (ii) - (q) ; (iii) - (p)
D). (i) - (q) ; (ii) - (p) ; (iii) - (r)

Q 7. By which of the following method, edge stiffening can be done ,
A). Wiring
B). Flanging
C). Curling
D). All of these

Q 8. Which of the following is not a purpose of edge stiffening
A). To give extra strength and rigidity to edges
B). To provide sharp edges for safe handling
C). To prevent edges from bending /buckling
D). To prevent edges from damage during handling.

Q 9. ________________ is a piece of material, which is cut to the exact size and shape, to form the desired object.
A). Pattern
B). Layout
C). Stretchout
D). Section

Q 10. Punches are made of __________.

A). stainless steel

B). tool steel

C). mild steel

D). cast iron

Q 11. Which of the following is not a part of Rivet

A). Head

B). Body

C). Tail

D). Tang

Q 12. ____________rivet is used to reduce the height of the rivet head above the metal surface.

A). Mushroom head

B). Snap head

C). Pan head

D). Countersunk head

Q 13. Identify the rivet as shown in figure -

A). Pan head

B). Countersunk head

C). Snap head

D). Mushroom head

Q 15. In soldering, ______________ is mainly used as flux for stainless steel.

A). Phosphoric acid

B). Hydrochloric acid

C). Zinc chloride

D). Ammonium chloride

Q 16. Which type of solder is used for soldering brass, copper and jewellery

A). Common solder

B). Coarse solder

C). Fine solder

D). Extra fine solder

Q 18. Melting point of silver solder is _____.

A). 350°C

B). 400°C

C). 600°C

D). 850°C

Q 19. Tank of Blow lamp is made of ________.

A). bronze

B). brass

C). mild steel

D). cast iron

Q 20. Identify the component X of Blow lamp as shown in figure -

A). Pressure release valve

B). Support bracket

C). Filler cap

D). Burner housing

Q 21. Identify the type of pipe joint as shown in figure -

A). Tee joint

B). Branch joint

C). L elbow joint L

D). Y joint Y

Q 22. Rotary shears are designed to cut sheet metal along ________ by a pair of rotary cutters, which rotate and produce a continuous cuting action.

A). straight line

B). circle

C). curved lines

D). straight line, circle and curved lines

Q 23. Which of the following is not a measuring tool

A). Try square

B). Steel rule

C). Trammel

D). Micrometer

Q 24. The accuracy of measurement by a try square is about _____ per 10 mm length.

A). 0.001 mm

B). 0.002 mm

C). 0.005 mm

D). 0.010 mm

Q 25. In combination set, ___________ can be rotated and set to any required angle.

A). Square head

B). Protractor head

C). Centre head

D). Rule

Q 26. The size of dividers ranges from ____________.

A). 50 mm to 100 mm

B). 50 mm to 200 mm

C). 50 mm to 300 mm

D). 50 mm to 600 mm

Q 28. In Oxy-acetylene gas welding, oxygen cylinder can store gas to a capacity of ____with the pressure ranging between _________.

A). 7 m3 ; 120-150 kg /cm2

B). 6 m3 ; 15-16 kg /cm2

C). 7 m3 ; 12-15 kg /cm2

D). 6 m3 ; 150-160 kg /cm2

Q 30. In which position the acetylene cylinder should keep while doing oxy acetylene gas welding

A). Straight upright

B). Horizontal

C). In inclined position

D). None of these

Q 31. Identify the equipment as shown in figure -

A). Spark lighter

B). Electrode holder

C). Earth clamp

D). Tip cleaner

Q 32. The nozzle of gas welding blow pipe is made up of_________.

A). Copper

B). Iron

C). Brass

D). Aluminium

Q 33. Which of the following is a function of the flux in gas welding

A). Dissolving oxide

B). Cleaning

C). To prevent impurities

D). All of these

Q 34. What is the source of heat in arc welding

A). Friction

B). Voltage

C). Electricity

D). Gas

Q 35. The colour of oxygen gas cylinder is __________.

A). Green
B). Blue
C). Red
D). Black
Q 36. Which of the following is not a type of dovetail seam
A). Plain
B). Flange
C). Slip
D). Beaded
Q 37. Aluminium fabrication is used in sheet metal work because -
A). It is light in weight
B). It is resistant to corrosion
C). It is easy to process
D). All of these
Q 39. Which of the following is not a property of aluminium
A). It readily dissolves in hydrochloric acid
B). Its specific gravity is about 2.7
C). It is a magnetic substance
D). It is a very good conductor of heat and electricity
Q 40. Melting point of copper is ______.
A). 1063 °C
B). 1083 °C
C). 660 °C
D). 2300 °C
Q 41. Which of the following is not an application of Aluminium
A). It is used as a reducing agent in the manufacture of steel
B). It is used in the casting of steel
C). It is used in the manufacture of electrical insulator
D). It is used in the manufacture of paints in powder form
Q 42. Which pattern development method is often used for Heating, ventilation, and air conditioning (HVAC) duct work
A). Parallel line method
B). Radial line method
C). Triangulation method
D). Geometrical construction method
Q 43. ______________ is used in explosives factories and petroleum refineries.______________
A). Pneumatic hand drill

B). Electric hand drill (light duty)

C). Electric hand drill (heavy duty)

D). All of these

Q 44. Which of the following synthetic soluble cutting oil is suitable for grinding iron, steel, non-alloyed and nickel chrome steel

A). SERVOSYNTH 2

B). SERVOSYNTH 3

C). SERVOSYNTH 4

D). SERVOSYNTH 5

Q 45. Press brake are designed to bend to a rated capacity depend upon a

die ratio of ______ , which is accepted as ideal condition.

A). 4:1

B). 6:1

C). 8:1

D). 10:1

Q 46. Correct sequence of operation during folding of sheet using bar folder are -- 1. Setting the work piece 2. Folding 3. Clamping 4. Removal of work

A). 1-2-3-4

B). 1-3-2-4

C). 1-2-4-3

D). 1-3-4-2

Q 47. In Universal swaging machine, ____________ is used to set the width of the flange and to guide the disc to get uniform flanging.

A). Locking nut for rollers

B). Set of rollers

C). Gauge plate with tightening screw

D). Upper roller adjusting handle

Q 48. Identify the operation carried out on Universal swaging machine as

shown in figure

A). Flanging

B). Burring

C). Flattening

D). Elbow edging

Q 49. In three roll forming machines, heavy gauge sheets and plates are formed by_____

A). Plain forming machine
B). Slip roll forming machine
C). Pyramid type roll forming machine
D). All of these

Q 50. In fly press, the rotary movement of the fly arm is converted into the __________ movement of the arm.
A). oscillating
B). translatory
C). reciprocating
D). circular

Q 51. Which of the following jig can be used while drilling small piece part
A). Solid jig
B). Post jig
C). Table jig
D). Sandwich jig

Q 52. Screwdrivers are available in many sizes, ranging from blade length of _________.
A). 25 mm to 500 mm
B). 30 mm to 300 mm
C). 30 mm to 500 mm
D). 25 mm to 300 mm

Q 53. Which of the following glass is used in the manufacture of artificial gems, electric bulbs, lenses and prisms
A). Potash-lead glass
B). Potash-lime glass
C). Soda-lime glass
D). Common glass

Q 54. In DC welding, ___ of the heat is liberated from the positive end and ____ from the negative end respectively. |
A). 1/3 ; 2/3
B). 2/3 ; 1/3
C). 1/2 ; 1/2
D). 3/4 ; 1/4

Q 55. In AC welding transformer, AC main supply has
A). high ampere-low voltage
B). high voltage-low ampere
C). high ampere-high voltage

D). low volatge-low ampere

Q 56. In DC welding generator, ____________ is mounted on a shaft which rotates on suitable bearings arranged at its end.

A). Armature

B). Commutators

C). Carbon brushes

D). Prime mover

Q 57. Identify the welding defect as shown in figure -

A). Slag inclusion

B). Spatter

C). Blow-hole

D). Undercut

Q 58. The picture shows a symbol, what type of symbol is this

A). Square butt weld

B). Plug weld

C). Spot weld

D). Seam weld

Q 59. In TIG welding, the two commonly used inert gases are -

A). Argon and carbon dioxide

B). Argon and helium

C). Helium and carbon dioxide

D). carbon dioxide and nitrogen

Q 60. For TIG welding of stainless steel sheets, heat distribution at DCEP is -

A). Electrode - 67% and Work - 33%

B). Electrode - 33% and Work - 67%

C). Electrode - 50% and Work - 50%

D). Electrode - 75% and Work - 25%

Q 61. Melting point of pure tungsten is ______.

A). 3380 °C

B). 1083 °C

C). 1768 °C

D). 3017 °C

Q 62. Edge machining allowance in laser cutting is ________.

A). 9.52 mm

B). 5.08 mm

C). 1.27 mm

D). 2.03 mm

Q 63. Which of the following material cannot be cut with water jet cutting

A). Tempered glass

B). Plastic

C). Stone

D). Leather

Q 64. Which of the following command is not related to DRAW TOOL

A). Line

B). Polygon

C). Rectangle

D). Chamfer

Q 65. The toolbar at the top of the AutoCAD 2008 window is-

A). Standard toolbar

B). Draw toolbar

C). Modify toolbar

D). Properties toolbar

Q 66. In AutoCAD, press the F9 key of the keyboard for_______

A). Snap on/off

B). Grid on/off

C). Ortho on/off

D). Osnap on/off

Q 67. What is the aim of first aid

A). Preserve life

B). Prevent harm

C). Promote recovery

D). All of these

Q 68. What is the use of dolly block in sheet metal

A). Shaping sheet metal

B). Joining sheet metal

C). Hammering sheet metal

D). Checking sheet metal

Q 69. Identify the tool shown in the figure.

A). Try square

B). File

C). Chisel

D). Steel rule

Q 70. Which of the following is a heating technique used in sheet metal works

A). Blow Lamp

B). LPG

C). Hand Forging

D). All of these

Q 71. Sheet metal work is carried out only on metal sheets, which are___________

A). Rolled

B). Forged

C). Cast

D). Moulded

Q 72. Which one of the following sheets is used for making highly corrosive acid tanks

A). Lead sheets

B). Black iron sheets

C). Galvanised iron sheets

D). Stainless steel sheets

Q 73. Cathodic and anodic protection are the techniques in which we protect the metal from____________

A). Corrosion

B). Melting

C). Bending

D). Twisting

Q 74. An oxidising process used for aluminium and magnesium articles is called ____________

A). Anodizing

B). Galvanising

C). Cyaniding

D). Sherardising

Q 75. What is the name of joint made by fastening two edges of sheet metal together

A). Seam

B). Grooved

C). Hem

D). Pane

Q 76. Allowance for knocked-up-joint is________

A). K=2W+2T

B). K=2W+3T

C). K=3W+2T

D). K=4W+6T

Q 77. If d=diameter of wire and t=thickness of sheet metal, then wiring allowance is equal to__________

A). 2.5 x d + t

B). 2.5 + d x t

C). 2.5 x d + 2t

D). 2.5 x d + 4t

Q 78. What is considered to be center while developing in the radial line method

A). Apex

B). Axis

C). Base

D). Surface

Q 79. Components which can not be developed either by parallel line method or radial line method or triangulation method can be easily developed by __________

A). Geometrical construction methods

B). Approximate method

C). Zone method

D). Line method

Q 80. Punches are specified by their__________

A). Diameter

B). Cutting edge

C). Cross section

D). Cutting angle

Q 82. Which material is used for solder

A). Pure metal or alloy

B). Non metallic element

C). Synthetic element

D). None of these

Q 83. Which flux is used for soldering, which is used in form of powder and evaporates when heating

A). Ammonium chloride

B). Hydrochloric acid

C). Zinc chloride

D). Phosphoric acid

Q 84. The plan is divided into how many parts to develop the pattern for a 90 elbow of equal diameter pipes by parallel line method

A). 12
B). 15
C). 20
D). 22

Q 85. Pipe less than 12 mm diameter is called ____________

A). Tube
B). Pipe
C). Socket
D). Cross

Q 86. Which tool is used for setting 1/8", 5/32" and 3/16" diameter standard open type rivets 1/8 ", 5/32" 3/16"

A). Lazy tong
B). Open break stem
C). Drive pin rivets
D). Sealed

Q 87. In an Oxy acetylene gas plant, the fuel gas used is____________

A). Acetylene
B). Oxygen
C). Hydrogen
D). LPG

Q 88. How many types of flames are there in oxy acetylene gas welding

A). 3
B). 2
C). 5
D). 4

Q 89. Which of the following welding process is shown in picture below

A). Arc welding
B). Submerged arc welding
C). Thermite welding
D). Flash butt welding

Q 90. Which of the following welding accessory is shown in picture below

A). Earth clamp
B). Electrode holder
C). Earth cable
D). C-clamp C-

Q 91. Which of the following welding accessory is shown in picture below

A). Gas cutting torch

B). Gas welding torch

C). MIG welding torch

D). TIG welding torch

Q 92. The arc utilized in an electric arc welding is -

A). Low voltage, high current discharge

B). Low voltage, low current discharge

C). High voltage, high current discharge

D). High voltage, low current discharge

Q 93. Manual metal arc welding is also known as ________

A). SMAW

B). GMAW

C). GTAW

D). FCAW

Q 94. Which one of the following is a safety device used in gas welding plant

A). Flash back arrestor

B). Blow pipe

C). Acetylene gas generator

D). None of these

Q 95. Which of the following is not a type of dovetail seam

A). Plain

B). Flange

C). Slip

D). Beaded

Q 96. Which of the following is not an application of Aluminium

A). It is used as a reducing agent in the manufacture of steel

B). It is used in the casting of steel

C). It is used in the manufacture of electrical insulator

D). It is used in the manufacture of paints in powder form

Q 97. Which of the following statement is true about aluminium

A). It is ductile metal

B). It is non-magnetic

C). Aluminium oxide has a higher melting point than aluminium

D). All of these

Q 98. Brass is an alloy of copper and ___________

A). Aluminium

B). Zinc

C). Tin

D). Steel

Q 99. Punching a number of holes in a sheet is known as____________

A). Perforating

B). Parting

C). Notching

D). Lancing

Q 100. Punches are made of __________

A). Stainless steel

B). Tool steel

C). Mild steel

D). Cast iron

Q 101. Which of the following is the operating principle of hydraulic pipebending machine

A). It uses kinetic energy to operate.

B). It uses hydraulic power to operate.

C). It uses atomic power to operate

D). None of these

Q 102. The operation of bending a sheet metal along a curved axis, is also known as________

A). Forming

B). Plunging

C). Notching

D). Slitting

Q 103. Fixture is a device which____________

A). Holds the workpiece

B). Locates the workpiece

C). Holds and locates the workpiece

D). Neither holds nor locates the workpiece

Q 104. Which one of the following is an element of jig

A). Base

B). Tool guiding frame

C). Body

D). All of these

Q 105. The operation of straightening a curved sheet metal, is known as_________

A). Planishing
B). Drawing
C). Squeezing
D). Coining

Q 106. which one of the following is the type of transformer used in arc welding

A). Step down
B). Step up
C). One-to-one
D). Capable of increasing supply voltage

Q 107. The heat generated (H) in resistance welding is expressed by__________.

A). I2RT
B). 2IRT
C). IR2T
D). IRT2

Q 108. Which of the following welding process is shown in picture below

A). Spot Welding
B). Seam welding
C). Projection Welding
D). Flash butt Welding

Q 109. Which of the following welding accessory is shown in picture below

A). CO2 welding torch CO2
B). Oxy-acetylene gas cutting torch
C). Oxy-acetylene gas welding torch
D). TIG welding torch

Q 110. Which of the following inert gas is used in MIG welding

A). Argon
B). Xenon
C). Carbon dioxide
D). Nitrogen

Q 111. Which of the following is another name of MIG welding

A). CO2 welding CO2
B). MAG welding
C). TIG welding
D). Submerged arc welding

Q 112. Which of the following is an advantage of MIG welding

A). Thick and thin material can be welded

B). Welding in all positions can be done

C). Deposition rate is high

D). All of these

Q 113. The selection of wire electrode to be used in CO2 welding will depend upon which factor

A). Joint design

B). Composition of metal being welded

C). The process being used

D). All of these

Q 114. What is the full form of term "TIG" in TIG welding

A). Tungsten inert gas

B). Torch inert gas

C). Tungsten inert gasoline

D). Tungsten inner gas

Q 115. Name the welding process shown in the picture.

A). TIG

B). MIG

C). MAG

D). MMAW

Q 116. Which of the following is an advantage of Pulsed TIG welding

A). Less distortion

B). Better penetration with less heat

C). Both less distortion and better penetration with less heat

D). None of these

Q 117. Which of the following is a reason of undercut in TIG welding

A). Unclean workpiece surface

B). Welding current too high

C). Insufficient shielding gas

D). All of these

Q 118. There is a standard colour indication for tungsten electrodes. Pure tungsten is marked with_______ colour

A). green

B). black

C). red

D). blue

Q 119. In straight polarity of TIG welding, _______% of the heat goes to the electrode end.

A). 30
B). 50
C). 70
D). 100

Q 120. Identify the welding joint shown in the figure.
A). Tee joint
B). Corner joint
C). Butt joint
D). Lap joint

Q 121. Which of the following is weld symbol for fillet joint
A). 30
B). 50
C). 70
D). 100

Q 122. Edge machining allowance in laser cutting is _______
A). 9.52 mm
B). 5.08 mm
C). 1.27 mm
D). 3.03 mm

Q 123. Which of the following is an advantage of plasma cutting
A). All metals and non-metals can be cut.
B). Cutting is possible in all positions.
C). Low cost of cutting
D). All of these

Q 124. Which of the following material cannot be cut with water jet cutting
A). Tempered glass
B). Plastic
C). Stone
D). Leather

Q 125. Identify the aluminium section shown in the figure.
A). Aluminium channel
B). Aluminium angle
C). Aluminium I-Beam
D). Aluminium T-Beam

Q 126. 6061, 6082, 5083, 5086, 5052, 6063, 7075, 1100 are the _______ of the Angle, Channel, Beam, and chains.
A). Specifications

B). Serial numbers

C). Random numbers

D). None of these

Q 127. Primers are used

A). Before painting

B). After painting

C). Together with paint

D). After drying the paint

Q 128. On which axis we do not work while make a drawing in 2D

A). Z

B). X

C). Y

D). WCS

Q 129. AutoCAD can be opened by________

A). left-click on the AutoCAD shortcut icon in the Windows desktop

B). Typing "acad" at the keyboard

C). Automatically when the computer is switched on

D). Selecting from a list which appears on screen when the computer is switched on

Q 1. __________ is used as a longitudinal corner seam for various types of pipes such as duct work.

A). Grooved seam

B). Pittsburgh seam

C). Dovetail seam

D). Pane down seam

Q 2. The hand groover is made up of __________ and is used to make______ grooved joint.

A). cast steel, internal locked

B). cast iron, external locked

C). cast steel, external locked

D). cast iron, internal locked

Q 3. Which of the following is not an advantage of false wiring

A). Cost of the article is reduced

B). Weight of the article is reduced

C). It helps to maintain the sides in position

D). Weight of the article is increased

Q 4. The stretchout of a round pipe is the________________ of the pipe.

A). Area

B). circumference
C). diameter
D). radius

Q 6. Identify the component X of Hand lever punch as shown in figure
A). Die
B). Punch holder
C). Throat
D). Gauge

Q 7. Formula generally used in the shop floor for determining the length of snap head rivet is - (where L=shank length, T=total thickness of the number of plates used and D= rivet diameter)
A). L=T+1.5D
B). L=T+0.6D
C). L=T+2.5D
D). L=T+2D

Q 8. Which clip is generally used for connecting cross seams on ducts
A). Government clip
B). Drive clip
C). Nailing clip
D). S clip S

Q 9. Identify the type of self tapping screw as shown in figure
A). Type-A
B). Type-B
C). Type-C
D). Type-D

Q 10. Which of the following is not a Semi-Permanent Treatmen
A). Galvanising
B). Tinning
C). Cladding
D). Anodising

Q 11. ________________ is used to provide a decorative and corrosion resistant coating on aluminium and its alloys only.
A). Electroplating
B). Anodising
C). Cladding
D). Galvanising

Q 12. _____________ is used for scribing circles, arcs and for transforming and stepping off distances.

A). Trammel
B). Radius gauge
C). Wing compass
D). Screw pitch gauge

Q 13. _______________ is used for the internl side cutting of an intricated work. ____

A). Aviation shear
B). Bench shear
C). Hawk Billed shear
D). Double cutting shear

Q 14. Which of the following sheet metal hammer is used in raising operation

A). Riveting hammer
B). Stretching hammer
C). Creasing hammer
D). Planishing hammer

Q 15. Identify the type of spanner as shown in figure -

A). Ring spanner
B). Adjustable spanner
C). Socket spanner
D). Hook spanner

Q 17. _______________ is used for drilling small diameter holes upto 6 mm.

A). Bevel gear type drilling machine
B). Ratchet drilling machine
C). Breast drilling machine
D). None of these

Q 18. Identify the drilling machine as shown in figure

A). Bevel gear type drilling machine
B). Ratchet drilling machine
C). Breast drilling machine
D). Pneumatic hand drilling machine

Q 21. Identify the component no. 6 of Universal swaging machine as shown in figure

A). Locking nut for rollers
B). Set of rollers
C). Upper shaft with gear
D). Lower shaft with gear

Q 22. _______________ is used for forming the neck of a vessel after initial drawing. _____

A). Core die

B). Segmental die

C). Outside drawing die

D). Inside drawing die

Q 23. Identify the press as shown in figure

A). Straight side press

B). Pillar press

C). Adjustable bed press

D). Gap press

Q 24. _____________ is the operation of forming the edge of an article into a roll. ___

A). Forming

B). Curling

C). Plunging

D). Cupping

Q 25. Which of the following is not a method of Polishing a metal by machine

A). Polishing with pedestal grinder

B). Polishing with compounds and cloth wheels

C). Polishing with abrasive covered wheels

D). Polishing with coated abrasive

Q 26. Which of the following buffing material is a powdered lava, white in colour used for scrubbing, cleaning and polishing

A). Tripoli

B). Pumice

C). Rouge

D). Whiting

Q 27. Identify the jig as shown in figure -

A). Solid jig

B). Post jig

C). Trunnion jig

D). Box jig

Q 28. In pipe bending machines, inner formers, lever, adjusting screw with lock nut and pipe guide are parts of ________

A). Bench type hand operated pipe bender

B). Portable hand operated pipe bender

C). Hydraulic bending machine

D). None of these

Q 30. Which type of welding is widely used in attaching fasteners to structural members

A). Spot welding

B). Seam welding

C). Projection welding

D). Flash butt welding

Q 31. Which of the following is not the equipment and accessories used for CO2 welding

A). Wire reel

B). Conduit linear

C). Force mechanism

D). Wire feed drive motor

Q 32. CO2 welding process cannot be used for welding ___________.

A). silicon

B). aluminium

C). zinc

D). copper

Q 33. Which of the following is not the advantage of argon as shielding gas

A). Low arc voltage

B). Easy arc starting

C). Small heat affected zone

D). Low gas volume

Q 34. In air plasma cutting, __________ electrode is used where dry, clean compressed air is used as the cutting gas.

A). tungsten

B). argon

C). helium

D). zirconium

Q 35. In the coordinate system of AutoCAD 2008

A). Positive X figures are to the right

B). Positive X figures are to the left

C). Positive figures are in the direction vertically upwards

D). Positive figures are in the direction vertically downwards

Q 36. Water is used to extinguish__________.

A). Class-A fires

B). Class-B fires

C). Class-C fires

D). Class-D fires

Q 39. What is Galvanising

A). Process of coating zinc by hot dipping

B). Zinc diffusion process

C). Process used for making thin phosphate coating on steel

D). All of these

Q 40. Which seam is used in sheet metal joint for roofing and panelling

A). Double grooved seam

B). Lap seam

C). Double seam

D). Grooved seam

Q 41. A piece of material which is cut to the exact size and shape to form the desired object is called __________

A). Pattern

B). Templates

C). Stretchout

D). Development

Q 42. The term______________ refers to the sizes of flat piece of metal before it is formed into shape.

A). Stretchout

B). Free hand sketch

C). Actual size

D). Development of surface

Q 43. Which of the following is not possible with the parallel line method

A). Pyramid

B). Cube

C). Prism

D). Cylinder

Q 44. Which of the following is a method of dividing the surface of the object in traingles

A). Triangulation method

B). Geometrical construction methods

C). Parallel line method

D). Radial line method

Q 45. Which type of punches have hollow cross-section

A). Hollow punch
B). Solid punch
C). Number punch
D). Letter punch
Q 46. Which type of rivet is used in heavy structural work
A). Pan head rivet
B). Snap head rivet
C). Counter sunk rivet
D). Conical head rivet
Q 47. Identify the rivet as shown in figure
A). Pan head
B). Countersunk head
C). Snap head
D). Mushroom head
Q 48. The government clip are sometimes also called___________
A). Cup or Pocket Clip
B). Nailing Clip
C). Drive Clip
D). S-Clip
Q 49. Which clip is generally used for connecting cross seams on ducts
A). Drive Clip
B). S-Clip
C). Government Clip
D). Nailing Clip
Q 50. Which of the following solder is the alloy of copper, tin, silver, zinc, cadmium and phosphorus
A). Hard solders
B). Soft solders
C). Medium solders
D). Zinc solders
Q 51. Generally which method is used for developing the pattern for a 90
elbow of equal diameter pipes
A). Parallel line method
B). Radial line method
C). Triangulation method
D). Geometrical construction methods
Q 52. Identify the type of pipe joint as shown in figure

A). <u>Tee joint</u>
B). Branch joint
C). L elbow joint L
D). Y joint Y
Q 53. The thickness of pipe is__________the tube.
A). <u>Greater than</u>
B). Less than
C). Equal to
D). Half the diameter of
Q 54. Which machine changes AC supply to DC in arc welding
A). Transformer
B). Blow pipe
C). <u>Welding rectifier</u>
D). Amplifier
Q 55. The flux commonly used in brazing is___________
A). <u>Borax</u>
B). Zinc chloride
C). Ammonium chloride
D). Copper Sulphate
Q 56. The coated electrodes used in arc welding. This coating is not for_______
A). <u>Preventing electrode from heat</u>
B). Adding alloying elements
C). Stabilize the arc
D). Providing protective atmosphere to weld
Q 57. Arc blow is more common in __________.
A). <u>DC welding</u>
B). AC welding
C). AC welding with bare electrodes
D). AC welding and DC welding both
Q 58. What is the name of machine shown in the figure below
A). Pillar drill machine
B). Bench Drill machine
C). <u>Hand Drill Machine</u>
D). None of these
Q 59. The cutting lip angle of a twist drill is_______
A). <u>118°</u>
B). 110°

C). 90°

D). 59°

Q 60. What is the name of machine shown in the figure below

A). Hydraulic pipe bending machine

B). Bench Drill machine

C). Projection Welding machine

D). None of these

Q 61. Which one of the following hand cutting tool is used for making inside threads in cylindrical holes

A). Tap

B). Die

C). Punch

D). All of these

Q 62. Which of the following is not a method of polishing a metal bymachine

A). Polishing with pedestal grinder

B). Polishing with compounds and cloth wheels

C). Polishing with abrasive covered wheels

D). Polishing with coated abrasive

Q 63. Which machine changes AC supply to DC supply in arc welding

A). Transformer

B). Blow pipe

C). Welding rectifier

D). None of these

Q 64. Which of the following is an effect of long arc

A). Less spatter

B). More fusion

C). More spatter

D). None of these

Q 65. Which of the following is not a type of resistance welding

A). MIG welding

B). Spot Welding

C). Seam welding

D). Projection Welding

Q 66. Which of the following welding process uses non-consumable electrodes

A). TIG welding

B). MIG welding

C). Manual arc welding

D). Submerged arc welding

Q 67. Which one of the following is a press tool

A). Blanking Tool

B). Trimming Tool

C). Drawing Tool

D). All of these

Q 68. Snips are also called as_______________.

A). Hand Shears

B). Lever shear

C). Stakes

D). Mallets

Q 69. What is the reason behind painting of vehicle

A). To prevent rust from growing on the body vehicles

B). To improve its external appearance

C). To retain the characteristics of steel for long time

D). All of these

Q 70. Powder coating is a type of coating that is applied as a free-flowing, ____

A). Dry powder

B). Liquid paint

C). Moisture

D). Water

Q 71. The commands Erase, Copy, Mirror, Trim, Extend, Break etc. belongs to which tool bar

A). Modify toolbar

B). Layer toolbar

C). Style toolbar

D). Draw toolbar

Q 72. Which command is used to create a round corner between two lines

A). Fillet

B). Chamfer

C). Stretch

D). Extend

Q 90] As the thickness of the material to be welded by arc welding increases, the welding current required

A] Increases

B] Decreases
C] Remains the same
D] May increase or decrease
Q 91] The type of current preferred for welding non-ferrous metal is
A] High frequency alternating current
B] Low frequency alternating current
C] Direct current
D] No preference
Q 92] The material used for coating of electrodes is called
A] Slag
B] Flux
C] Sticker
D] Binder
Q 93] Is it OK to wear nylon clothing when doing welding?
A] No, it causes too much sweating
B] No, it can catch fire easily
C] It's fine, you can wear it
D] No, because it can create static electricity and cause shock
Q 94] Acetylene can be prepared by chemical reaction between
A] Water and calcium carbide
B] Water and calcium carbonate
C] Hydrogen and calcium carbide
D] Hydrogen and calcium carbonate
Q 95] How is the size of an arc welding electrode specified?
A] By its weight
B] By the metal it is required to weld
C] By its current carrying capacity
D] By its overall diameter
Q 96] Which material can be best cut by oxy-acetylene cutting?
A] Brass
B] Cast iron
C] Mild steel
D] Aluminium
Q 97] The gas which is supporter of combustion is
A] Oxygen
B] Hydrogen
C] Carbon dioxide
D] Acetylene

Q 98] The entrapment of gas in the weld causes the defect
A] Lack of fusion
B] Cracks
C] Porosity
D] Slag inclusion
Q 99] As a matter of safety, one should not do arc welding
A] While standing on wet floor
B] In poor lighted area
C] When someone standing nearby
D] In well ventilated confined area
Q 100] What may happen if oil or grease is used on gas regulator?
A] Oil or grease may burn
B] Regulator may burn
C] Cylinder may explode
D] All of these
Q 101] The original metal being joined by welding is called
A] Bare metal
B] Bead metal
C] Base metal
D] Raw metal
Q 102] Which statement is not true about MIG welding?
A] The speed of welding is high
B] There is no slag to be removed
C] The welds produced are sound
D] Electric arc is not visible to the operator
Q 103] In electrode-positive welding , ...of total heat is produced at the electrode]
A] Two-third
B] One-third
C] One-half
D] One-fourth
Q 104] What medium is used to dissolve acetylene?
A] Water
B] Acetone
C] Jelly
D] Calcium hydroxide
Q 105] A cylinder which contains acetylene is painted
A] Blue

B] Black

C] Maroon

D] Brown

Q 106] The term used to indicate amount of current flowing in a circuit is

called]]]]]]]]

A] Ohm

B] Ampere

C] Farad

D] Volt

Q 107] What should be used to clean the tip orifice of gas cutting torch?

A] Tip cleaner

B] Steel wire

C] Copper wire

D] Small drill

Q 108] Which weld defect can be easily detected by visual examination?

A] Lack of side wall fusion

B] Root defect in a T fillet joint

C] Slag inclusion

D] Misalignment of parts

Q 109] Which one of these metals has the highest thermal conductivity?

A] Aluminium

B] Copper

C] Zinc

D] Steel

distortion

Q 110] Two plates being welded get pulled towards each other and the angle between them changes from the originally set angle] The distortion caused is called

A] Universal distortion

B] Longitudinal distortion

C] Angular distortion

D] Transverse distortion

Q 111] Which testing method can be hazardous to the operator?

A] X - ray test

B] Ultrasonic test

C] Liquid penetrant test

D] Magnetic particle test

Q 112] Which of these is a non-destructive test?

A] Impact test

B] Nick break test

C] Tensile test

D] Hydraulic pressure test

Q 113] The melting point of medium carbon steel is

A] 1510 degree C

B] 1426 degree C

C] 1305 degree C

D] 1082 degree C

Q 114] The last bit of unused electrode is called

A] Waste end

B] Discard end

C] Stub end

D] Little end

Q 115] What is used to conduct current from welding cable to electrode?

A] Earth cable

B] Electrode holder

C] Earth clamp

D] Cable lug

Q 116] What is the open circuit voltage of a welding transformer?

A] 90 V

B] 110 V

C] 130 V

D] 150 V

Q 117] The welding machine which can supply both AC and DC]

A] Engine driven welding generator

B] Motor driven welding generator

C] Welding transformer

D] Welding rectifier

Q 118] For gas cutting of 6 mm thick mild steel plate, what should be the size of the nozzle?

A] 0]4 mm

B] 0]6 mm

C] 0]8 mm

D] 1]0 mm

Q 119] The function of gas regulator is ....

A] To mix gases in required proportion

B] To set the working pressure

C] To get different types of flames

D] To change the volume of gas flowing through the blowpipe

Q 120] What edge preparation should be used for welding of 12 mm thick

MS plate?

A] Single

B] Double

C] Single

D] No bevelling

Q 121] It is easiest to weld in ....

A] Horizontal position

B] Vertical position

C] Overhead position

D] Downhand position

Q 122] Which fuel gas gives maximum flame temperature?

A] Acetylene

B] Coal gas

C] Hydrogen

D] Liquid petroleum gas

Q 123] Spatter during arc welding happens due to ....

A] High welding current

B] Use of damp electrodes

C] Use of short arc

D] Arc blow

Q 124] What is the purpose of water supply in TIG welding?

A] Cool the job

B] Wash the torch

C] Avoid distortion

D] Cool the torch

Q 125] The distance from work surface to the top of the weld bead is called ....

A] Bead width

B] Reinforcement

C] Penetration

D] Fusion zone

Q 126] If the weld does not combine with another weld or the base metal,

it is referred to as ....

A] Incomplete fusion

B] Incomplete bonding

C] Incomplete penetration

D] Incomplete inclusion

Q 127] Vapours of lead, zinc and cadmium ....

A] Can be ignored

B] Are highly flammable

C] Are hazardous

D] May cause slag inclusion

Q 128] Normally acetylene should be discharged from a cylinder at a rate which will empty it in not less than ....

A] 2 hours

B] 5 hours

C] 8 hours

D] 10 hours

Q 129] The type of electrodes which pick up moisture easily is

A] Acidic coated electrodes

B] Basic coated electrodes

C] Rutile coated electrodes

D] Titanium coated electrodes

Q 1] Identify the welding joint shown in the picture]

A] Tee joint

B] Corner joint

C] Butt joint

D] Lap joint

Q 2] Combustion of oxy-acetylene flame produces about ________ degree

centigrade temperature]

A] 2400 to 2700

B] 1800 to 2200

C] 3100 to 3300

D] 1825 to 1875

Q 3] Acetylene gas is composed of carbon and ____________

A] argon

B] nitrogen

C] oxygen

D] Hydrogen

Q 4] The color of the acetylene gas cylinder is _____

A] green

B] black

C] maroon

D] Blue

Q 5] Which gas cylinder is also called as DA gas cylinder?

A] Acetylene gas cylinder

B] Oxygen gas cylinder

C] Argon gas cylinder

D] None of these

Q 6] 1 volume of liquid acetone can dissolve _______ volume of acetylene

gas under normal atmospheric pressure and temperature]

A] 10

B] 20

C] 25

D] 30

Q 7] Which one of the following is a type of gas regulator used in oxyacetylene

gas welding?

A] Single stage regulator

B] Double stage regulator

C] Both single and double stage regulator

D] None of these

Q 8] Identify the equipment shown in the picture]

A] Gas regulator

B] Welding blowpipe

C] Tip cleaner

D] Spark lighter

Q 9] In oxy acetylene gas cutting torch,the angle of the cutting nozzle with the body is ___ degree]

A] 45

B] 60

C] 90

D] 120

Q 10] In oxy acetylene gas welding blowpipe, the angle of the welding nozzle with the neck is ___ degree]

A] 45

B] 60

C] 90

D] 120

Q 11] How many control valves a welding blowpipe has, to control the flame?

A] 1
B] 2
C] 3
D] 4
Q 12] Leftward welding technique is also called as ______]
A] forward technique
B] backward technique
C] backhand technique
D] interior technique
Q 13] One function of flux in gas welding is ________]
A] to merge metal oxide
B] to reduce the melting point of the metal
C] to increase the temperature of flame
D] to clean hose pipe
Q 14] The liquid temperature of the filler metal used in brazing is more than________ degree centigrade]
A] 150
B] 450
C] 723
D] 100
Q 15] The size of cutting nozzle used in oxy- acetylene cutting process depends mainly on _____]
A] thickness of metal to be cut
B] purity of oxygen
C] duration of cut
D] type of cutting blowpipe
Q 16] Which of the following is a gas welding defect?
A] Crack
B] Porosity
C] Lack of fusion
D] All of these
Q 17] Which of the following is used to enlight the flame in oxy-acetylene
gas cutting?
A] Electrode holder
B] Electrode
C] Spark lighter
D] Tip cleaner

Q 18] What is the unit of electric current?
B] Ampere
C] Ohm
D] Meter
Q 19] The pressure which makes the electric current to flow is called ________]
A] Electric current
B] Electric resistance
C] Conductivity
D] Voltage
Q 20] Which machine changes AC supply to DC in arc welding?
A] Transformer
B] Blow pipe
C] Welding rectifier
D] None of these
Q 21] Which of the following is AC welding machine?
A] DC motor generator
B] AC welding transformer
C] Rectifier set
D] None of these
Q 22] Which of the following is a welding position?
A] Flat
B] 2F
C] 3G
D] All of these
Q 24] Which of the following is an effect of long arc?
A] Less spatter
B] More fusion
C] More spatter
D] None of these
Q 25] An imaginary line passing through the weld center lengthwise is known as__________]
A] Weld rotation
B] Weld bead
C] Weld slop
D] Axis of weld
Q 26] Straight polarity is also called as______]
A] DCEP

B] DCEN
C] MMAW
D] GMAW
Q 27] When the arc deviates from its regular path due to the magnetic disturbances it is called______]
A] arc blow
B] overlap
C] undercut
D] arc trap
Q 28] Tip orifice of blowpipe nozzle should be cleaned with ____]
A] soft copper wire
B] steel wire
C] a small drill
D] tip cleaner
Q 29] Which of the following safety instruments is used to protect the eyes while doing grinding?
A] Hand screen
B] Helmet
C] Chipping goggles
D] Chipping screen
Q 30] Value of flux coating factor for light coated electrode is_________
A] 1]25 to 1]3
B] 1]4 to 1]5
C] 1]8 to 2]2
D] more than 2]2
Q 31] Which of the following is a cause of undercut in welding?
A] Current too high
B] Current too low
C] Use of long arc
D] None of these
Q 32] The third digit of number 7018 in American electrode coding E7018
indicates ____________]
A] Tensile strength of the joint
B] Welding position
C] Type of flux coating
D] Welding current and voltage condition
Q 33] Which type of power source is used in gas metal arc welding?

A] Constant voltage
B] Constant current
C] Constant resistance
D] None of these
Q 34] Which of the following metal transfer mode in MIG welding is also called as dip transfer?
A] Spray transfer
B] Short circuit transfer
C] Globular transfer
D] None of these
Q 35] Which of the following is a part of wire feeder of GMA welding?
A] Drive moter
B] Drive roller
C] Wire spool holder
D] All of these
Q 36] The last digit in American coding of GMAW wire electrode E 70S-2
indicates _____]
A] Tensile strength of the joint
B] chemical composition of wire
C] Type of flux coating
D] Welding current and voltage condition
Q 37] In FCAW, the deposition efficiency is generally in between________]
A] 20% to 30%
B] 30% to 45%
C] 60% to 66%
D] 80% to 86%
Q 38] Which of the following gas is used for shielding purpose in GMAW apart from argon?
A] carbon dioxide
B] nitrogen
C] oxygen
D] Hydrogen
Q 39] Which type of power source is used in TIG welding?
A] Constant voltage
B] Constant current
C] Constant resistance

D] None of these

Q 40] Which part of the TIG welding torch holds the electrode?

A] Nozzle

B] Collet

C] Back cap

D] Lead

Q 41] Gas nozzle of torch used in gas tungsten arc welding is made of ______]

A] plastic

B] copper

C] glass

D] Ceramic

Q 42] Identify the equipment shown in the picture]

A] Gas regulator

B] Flowmeter

C] Collet

D] Torch

Q 43] Melting point of pure tungsten is approximately ______ degrees centigrade]

A] 2050

B] 2550

C] 2830

D] 3380

Q 44] Which of the following statement is true?

A] Argon is a colourless gas

B] Argon is heavier than helium

C] Helium is a colourless gas

D] All of these

Q 45] What is the purpose of inert gas used in TIG welding?

A] To protect the molten metal from the atmospheric contamination

B] To contaminate in the weld metal

C] To stabilize the Arc

D] To get more spatters

Q 46] Which of the following statement is not true about submerged arc welding?

A] No spattering occur in this welding]

B] Welding can be done in flat position]

C] Welding can be done in overhead position]

D] None of these

Q 47] The electrode used in the spot welding is made up of which metal?

A] Copper

B] Brass

C] Carbon

D] Aluminium

Q 48] Which of the following can be easily be welded from flash butt welding process?

A] Cast iron

B] Lead

C] Brass

D] Mild steel

Q 49] Projection welding and seam welding are the types of ________ welding]

A] Gas metal arc welding

B] TIG welding

C] Resistance welding

D] Friction welding

Q 50] Which of the following should be used to remove slag and oxide after welding cast iron?

A] Tip cleaner

B] Ball peen hammer

C] Wire brush

D] None of these

Q 51] What type of filler rod should be selected to prevent weld decay in

stainless steel welding?

A] Columbium base

B] Copper coated mild steel

C] Super silicon

D] None of these

Q 52] The preheating temperature of the workpiece can be checked by ________]

A] touching with finger

B] pyrometer

C] temperature indicating crayons

D] Thermocouple

Q 53] Which type of oxy-acetylene gas flame is used for gas welding of pure aluminium ?

A] Neutral

B] Carburising

C] Oxidising

D] None of these

Q 54] Which of the following is not a property of aluminium?

A] Good thermal conductivity

B] Good electrical conductivity

C] Light weight

D] Bad electrical conductivity

Q 55] Which of the following term is related to welding?

A] WPS

B] AWS

C] WPQ

D] All of these

Q 56] Izod and Charpy machines are related to ________ testing]

A] Impact

B] Ductility

C] Hardness

D] Creep

Q 57] Which quality of material can be tested with the help of Rockwell and Brinell test?

A] Hardness

B] Malleability

C] Elasticity

D] Ductility

Q 58] In dye penetrant test the penetrant passes into cracks by________Action]

A] capillary

B] friction

C] radiation

D] Conduction

Q 59] In which of the following test, sound waves of high frequency are used?

A] Pressure test

B] Impact test

C] Radiography test

D] Ultrasonic test

Q 60] Gamma rays are produced by__________]

A] Iridium

B] Cobalt 60

C] Titanium

D] Tungste

Q 61] Which metal alloy is used to make contact tip of MIG welding torch?

\ MIG

A] Copper

B] Aluminium

C] Mild steel

D] Zinc

Q 62] Which shielding gas is used in TIG welding?

A] Hydrogen

B] Nitrogen

C] Argon

D] Ozone

Q 63] Which of these is not a resistance welding process?

A] Projection welding

B] Seam welding

C] Flash butt welding

D] Carbon arc welding

Q 64] A single V edge preparation is used when plates .... thick are to be welded]

A] 1 to 5 mm

B] 5 to 15 mm

C] 15 to 25 mm

D] More than 25 mm

Q 65] The welding process which requires flux in granular form is ....

A] Gas welding

B] Submerged arc welding

C] Manual metal arc welding

D] Thermit welding

Q 66] The oxy-acetylene flame used for welding of aluminium is

A] Oxidizing flame

B] Neutral flame

C] Neutral flame with little haze of excess oxygen

D] Neutral flame with little haze of excess acetylene

Q 67] A device used to keep the parts to be welded in alignment is called

A] Welding jig

B] Welding fixture

C] Welding positioner

D] Welding manipulator

Q 68] The process which uses non-consumable electrode is ....

A] TIG

B] MIG

C] MAG

D] SAW

Q 69] What will happen if the blowpipe while gas cutting is moved to and

fro frequently?

A] The kerf will be narrow

B] The kerf will be wide

C] There will be no effect on the kerf

D] The kerf will be of correct size

Q 70] Cast iron can be best welded by ....

A] MIG welding

B] TIG welding

C] Arc welding

D] Gas welding

Q 71] What type of weld is obtained when two pieces of flat bar are joined to form T ?

A] Butt

B] Fillet

C] Lap

D] Edge

Q 72] Which type of non-destructive test is suitable to check the internal defects in high pressure boiler welding?

A] Radiographic test

B] Visual test

C] Magnetic particle test

D] Dye penetrant test

INDUSTRIAL TRAINING INSTITUTE

Monthly Test-1, Marks- 20, Date:- ________________

(Every Question Carry Two Marks)

16] Benefit of SS system is ------

A] Increase in productivity

B] Increase in quality

C] Reduction in wastage of time

D] All of these

17] Safety is -----------

A] nobody's business

B] every bodise business

C] Some bodies business

D] The organization business

18] For basic categories of safety signs are available The meaning of"prohibition" sign ----

A] shows it must not be done

B] Shows what must be done

C] Warns the hazard or danger

D] Gives information of safety provision

18] One micrometer (U] is equal to...

A] 0.1mm

B] 0.01mm

C] 0.001mm

D] 0.0001mm

19] The caliper meant for measuring the width of a slot is...

A] Odd leg caliper

B] Outside caliper

C] Jenny caliper

D] Inside calliper

20] The size of the dividers are specified by the -----------

A] Total length of legs

B] Distance between the points when fully opened

C] Length of legs without points

D] distance between the pivot and the point

21] The instrument used to mark parallel lines, parallel to the datum edge is -

A] jenny caliper

B] Divider

C] Outside calliper

D] Inside calliper

22] Which one of the following is an indirect measuring tool?

A] Outside caliper

B] Vernier calliper

C] Steel rule

D] Outside micrometer

23] For cutting thin tubing, the most suitable pitch of the hacksaw blade is...

A] 1.8mm

B] 1.4mm

C] 1mm

D] 0.8mm

24] For cutting solid brass, the most suitable pitch of the hacksaw blade is...

A] 1.8mm

B] 1.4mm

C] 1mm

D] 0.8mm

INDUSTRIAL TRAINING INSTITUTE

Monthly Test-2, Marks- 20, Date:- _______________

(Every Question Carry Two Marks)

31] Scribers are made of...

A] Mild steel

B] High carbon steel

C] Brass

D] Cast iron

32] Portion of the hammer used for fixing the handle is...

A] Face

B] Peen

C] Cheek

D] Eye hole

33] Weight of the hammer for the marking purpose is...

A] 250g

B] 500g

C] 1 kg

D] 2 kgs

Hammer

34] The size of the dividers are specified by the...

A] Total length of the legs

B] Distance between the points when fully opened

C] Length of legs without the points

D] Distance between the pivot and the point
35] The included angle of the groove of 'V' block is always....
A] 45◦
B] 60◦
C] 90◦
D] 120◦
36] 'V' blocks are available in grades of...
A] A & B
B] A,B & C
C] 1,2 & 3
D] 1 & 2
37] 'V' blocks of grade 'B' are made of
A] Cast iron
B] Mild steel
C] Steel
D] Cast steel
38] Name the punch used to locate the centre.
A] Prick punch 30°
B] Prick punch 60°
C] Centre punch
D] Dot punch
Centre punch
39] The point angle of centre punch is --------
A] 30°
B] 50°
c] 900
D] 1200
40] Punches are used for forming ---------of any shape
A] Holes
B] Mining
C] Knurling
D] Reaming

INDUSTRIAL TRAINING INSTITUTE

Monthly Test-3, Marks- 20, Date:- ______________

(Every Question Carry Two Marks)

50] A slight convexity is given to the cutting edge to...
A] Cut curved surfaces
B] Cut sharp corners

C] Prevent digging of the ends
D] Allow the lubricant to enter
51] Surface plates are made of...
A] High grade cast steel
B] Fine-grained cast iron
C] Alloy steels
D] Wrought iron
52] Surface plates are specified by their length and breadth & are in
A] decimetre
B] Cubic meter
C] Cylindrical
53] Ribs are given on the unmachined portion of the angle plate for...
A] Easy handling
B] Convenience in manufacturing
C] Clamping while setting on machines
D] Rigidity and to prevent distortion
54] The slots on the angle plate are given for...
A] Reducing weight
B] Aligning the work
C] Lifting using hooks
D] Accommodating bolts.
55] The size of the angle plates is stated by...
A] Weight
B] Length
C] Length x width
D] Size number
56] for high speed parting off work on material like cemented carbide Is'
A] Do all machine
B] Cutting off machine
C] Heavy duty power saw
D] Mining machine sitting saw
57] Gun metal is an alloy of copper, ------------
A] tin and zinc
B] Lead and zinc
C] Zinc and nickel
D] Lead and nickel
58] Cast iron is used for manufacturing machine beds because -------
A] it can resist more compressive stress

B] it is heavy in weight

C] It is cheaper metal

D] It is a brittle metal

59] Accuracy or least count of a metric outside micrometric is ---------

A] 0-1 mm

B] 0.01 mm

C] 0.001 mm

D] 0.02 mm

INDUSTRIAL TRAINING INSTITUTE

Monthly Test-4, Marks- 20, Date:- _______________

(Every Question Carry Two Marks)

70] The least count of a vernier bevel protractor is...

A] 1”

B] 5’

C] 1◦

D] 5 ◦

71] The part of a vernier bevel protractor which is normally used as a reference base for

measuring angles is the...

A] Blade

B] Stock

C] Disc

C] Main scale

72] The part of a vernier bevel protector on which main scale divisions are marked is the...

A] Stock

B] Dial

C] Disc

D] Adjustable blade

73] The part of a bevel protractor, which comes in contact with the inclined surface while

measuring is the...

A] Blade

B] Stock

C] Disc

D] Dial

74] The value of each division of the main scale of a vernier bevel protractor is...

A] 5’

B] 1◦

C] 5◦

D]10◦

75] The value of each division of the vernier scale of a bevel protractor is...

A] 1◦

B] 1◦5’

C] 1◦55’

D] 5’

76] The taper shank drills are held on the machine by means of...

A] Chucks

B] Sleeves

C] Drift

D] Vice

77] Drill chucks are fitted on the drilling machine spindle by means of a...

A] Knurled ring

B] Arbor

C] Drift

D] Pinion and key

78] The Morse taper provided on drills ranges between...

A] MT 1 to MT 5

B] MT 1 to MT 4

C] MT 0 to MT 5

D] MT 0 to MT 4

79] A drift is used for...

A] Drawing a drill location

B] Fixing chuck on the machine spindle

C] Removing a broken drill from the work

D] Removing the drill from the machine spindle

INDUSTRIAL TRAINING INSTITUTE

Monthly Test-5, Marks- 20, Date:- _______________

(Every Question Carry Two Marks)

90] Which one of the following drilling machine is used for heavy duty work?

A] Bench drilling machine

B] Pillar drilling machine

C] Radial drilling machine

D] Electric hand drilling machine

91] Drill chuck are held on the machine spindle by means of ------

A] arbor

B] Drift

C] draw-in bar

D] Chuck nut

92] Different speeds are obtained in a sensitive bench drilling machine by ----

A] Belt pulley mechanism

B] Hydraulic mechanism

C] Rack and Pinion mechanism

D] Cam and follower mechanism

103] Gun metal is an alloy of copper, ------------

A] tin and zinc

B] Lead and zinc

C] Zinc and nickel

D] Lead and nickel

104] for making gutters, roof flashing, hoods etc.

A] Galvanised iron

B] Stainless steel

C] Copper sheet

D] Metal sheets

105] in dairies. food processing, kitchen ware etc.

A] Galvanised iron

B] Stainless steel

C] Copper sheet

D] Metal sheets

106] for making buckets, heating ducts, cabinets etc.

A] Galvanised iron

B] Stainless steel

C] Copper sheet

D] Metal sheets

107] Punching a number of holes in a sheet is known as?

a) Perforating

b) Parting

c) Notching

d) Lancing

108] Shearing the sheet into two or more pieces is known as?

a) Perforating

b) Parting

c) Notching

d) Lancing

109] Removing the pieces from the edge in shearing operation is known as?

a) Perforating

b) Parting

c) Notching

d) Lancing

INDUSTRIAL TRAINING INSTITUTE

Monthly Test-6, Marks- 20, Date:- ______________

(Every Question Carry Two Marks)

182] Which one of the following is used only for finishing and maintaining correct form of

thread?

A] Tap

B] Threading tool

C] Threading chaser

D] Tipped tool

188] A die in which more than one cutting operation is per formed in one stroke

A] Piercing die

B] Progressive die

C] Combination die

D] Compound die

189] A die in which cutting and non cutting operations are carried out per stroke.

A] Piercing die

B] Progressive die

C] Combination die

D] Compound die

Tap Die

190] A die in which two or more sequential operations are performed at two or more stations

upon the work.

A] Piercing die

B] Progressive die

C] Combination die

D] Compound die

191] A die in which the shape of the punch and die are directly reproduced in the metal with

little or no metal flow.

A] Progressive die

B] Combination die

C] Compound die

D] Forming die

192] The die used for producing any shape of holes.

A] Piercing die

B] Progressive die

C] Combination die

D] Compound die

193] Abrasives are classifications into............

A] Two types

B] Three types

c] One types

D] Four types

194] Grinding wheels made out of---------------- abrasive are most common because of its free and

cool cutting action.

A] Aluminium oxide

B] Silicon oxide

C] Ammonium oxide

D] Carbide.

195] Which among the following abrasive is mostly used for cutting off wheels for cutting non

metallic materials?

A] Aluminium oxide

B] Silicon carbide

C] Diamond

D] None of above

196] Which abrasive particle is used for grinding tungsten carbide tool insert?

A] Silicon carbide

B] A|203

C] Diamond

D] Corundum

INDUSTRIAL TRAINING INSTITUTE

Monthly Test-7, Marks- 20, Date:- ______________

(Every Question Carry Two Marks)

200] What kind of abrasive cut of wheel should be used to cut concrete stone and masonry?

A] Silicon

B] Al203

C] Diamond grit

D] Glass

201] Aluminium oxide wheel is used for grinding ------------

A] cast iron

B] Cemented carbide.

C] HSS '

D] ceramic

202] The bond of diamond wheel suitable for offhand grinding of the tipped tool is ....

A] Resinoid

B] Vitrified

C] Shellac

D] Metal

Grinding Wheel

318] The number of threads per inch can be checked with a

A] tool gauge

B] metric rule by counting

C] ring gauge

D] screw pitch gauge

screw pitch gauge

319] When threading, the carriage is moved along the ways by

A] a gear train on a track

B] the feed rod spline or key-way

C] the lead screw thred

D] the hand wheel

320] Thread chasers are used for

A] quick production of threads

B] maintaining an exact form of thread

C] cutting threads on hard materials

D] cutting threads on soft materials

Q 1. Which of the following is not a cause of accident

A). Awareness of danger

B). Disregard for safety

C). Lack of understanding of proper safety procedures

D). Improper use of tools

Q 2. What is the first action, if your friend receives a heavy electric shock

A). Pull the friend from the live conductor

B). Pour water to avoid burning of friend

C). Fetch the first aid box

D). Switch off the current immediately

Q 3. Match the following - Safety Signs Shape

(i) Prohibition Sign (p) Triangular

(ii) Warning Sign (q) Square

(iii) Information (r) Data

A). (i) - (r) ; (ii) - (p) ; (iii) - (q)

B). (i) - (p) ; (ii) - (r) ; (iii) - (q)

C). (i) - (r) ; (ii) - (q) ; (iii) - (p)

D). (i) - (q) ; (ii) - (p) ; (iii) - (r)

Q 4. Identify the Warning Sign as shown in figure -

A). Risk of Explosion

B). Risk of Electric Shock

C). Risk of ionizing Radiation

D). Risk of Fire

INDUSTRIAL TRAINING INSTITUTE

Monthly Test-8, Marks- 20, Date:- ______________

(Every Question Carry Two Marks)

Q 10. Punches are made of ___________.

A). stainless steel

B). tool steel

C). mild steel

D). cast iron

Q 11. Which of the following is not a part of Rivet

A). Head

B). Body

C). Tail

D). Tang

Q 12. ____________rivet is used to reduce the height of the rivet head above the metal surface.

A). Mushroom head

B). Snap head

C). Pan head

D). Countersunk head

Q 13. Identify the rivet as shown in figure -

A). Pan head

B). Countersunk head

C). Snap head

D). Mushroom head

Q 15. In soldering, ______________ is mainly used as flux for stainless steel.

A). Phosphoric acid

B). Hydrochloric acid

C). Zinc chloride

D). Ammonium chloride

Q 16. Which type of solder is used for soldering brass, copper and jewellery

A). Common solder

B). Coarse solder

C). Fine solder

D). Extra fine solder

Q 18. Melting point of silver solder is _____.

A). 350°C

B). 400°C

C). 600°C

D). 850°C

Q 19. Tank of Blow lamp is made of ________.

A). bronze

B). brass

C). mild steel

D). cast iron

Q 20. Identify the component X of Blow lamp as shown in figure -

A). Pressure release valve

B). Support bracket

C). Filler cap

D). Burner housing

Q 21. Identify the type of pipe joint as shown in figure -

A). Tee joint

B). Branch joint

C). L elbow joint L

D). Y joint Y

INDUSTRIAL TRAINING INSTITUTE

Monthly Test-9, Marks- 20, Date:- ______________

(Every Question Carry Two Marks)

Q 30. In which position the acetylene cylinder should keep while doing oxy acetylene gas

welding

A). Straight upright

B). Horizontal

C). In inclined position

D). None of these

Q 31. Identify the equipment as shown in figure -

A). Spark lighter

B). Electrode holder

C). Earth clamp

D). Tip cleaner

Q 32. The nozzle of gas welding blow pipe is made up of__________.

A). Copper

B). Iron

C). Brass

D). Aluminium

Q 33. Which of the following is a function of the flux in gas welding

A). Dissolving oxide

B). Cleaning

C). To prevent impurities

D). All of these

Q 34. What is the source of heat in arc welding

A). Friction

B). Voltage

C). Electricity

D). Gas

Q 35. The colour of oxygen gas cylinder is ___________.

A). Green

B). Blue
C). Red
D). Black
Q 36. Which of the following is not a type of dovetail seam
A). Plain
B). Flange
C). Slip
D). Beaded
Q 37. Aluminium fabrication is used in sheet metal work because -
A). It is light in weight
B). It is resistant to corrosion
C). It is easy to process
D). All of these
Q 39. Which of the following is not a property of aluminium
A). It readily dissolves in hydrochloric acid
B). Its specific gravity is about 2.7
C). It is a magnetic substance
D). It is a very good conductor of heat and electricity
Q 40. Melting point of copper is ______.
A). 1063 °C
B). 1083 °C
C). 660 °C
D). 2300 °C

INDUSTRIAL TRAINING INSTITUTE
Monthly Test-10, Marks- 20, Date:- ______________
(Every Question Carry Two Marks)

Q 96. Which of the following is not an application of Aluminium
A). It is used as a reducing agent in the manufacture of steel
B). It is used in the casting of steel
C). It is used in the manufacture of electrical insulator
D). It is used in the manufacture of paints in powder form
Q 97. Which of the following statement is true about aluminium
A). It is ductile metal
B). It is non-magnetic
C). Aluminium oxide has a higher melting point than aluminium
D). All of these
Q 98. Brass is an alloy of copper and ____________
A). Aluminium

B). Zinc
C). Tin
D). Steel

Q 99. Punching a number of holes in a sheet is known as____________
A). Perforating
B). Parting
C). Notching
D). Lancing

Q 100. Punches are made of __________
A). Stainless steel
B). Tool steel
C). Mild steel
D). Cast iron

Q 101. Which of the following is the operating principle of hydraulic pipebending machine
A). It uses kinetic energy to operate.
B). It uses hydraulic power to operate.
C). It uses atomic power to operate
D). None of these

Q 102. The operation of bending a sheet metal along a curved axis, is also known as________
A). Forming
B). Plunging
C). Notching
D). Slitting

Q 103. Fixture is a device which____________
A). Holds the workpiece
B). Locates the workpiece
C). Holds and locates the workpiece
D). Neither holds nor locates the workpiece

Q 104. Which one of the following is an element of jig
A). Base
B). Tool guiding frame
C). Body
D). All of these

Q 105. The operation of straightening a curved sheet metal, is known as_________
A). Planishing

B). Drawing

C). Squeezing

D). Coining

INDUSTRIAL TRAINING INSTITUTE

Monthly Test-11, Marks- 20, Date:- ______________

(Every Question Carry Two Marks)

Q 115. Name the welding process shown in the picture.

A). TIG

B). MIG

C). MAG

D). MMAW

Q 116. Which of the following is an advantage of Pulsed TIG welding

A). Less distortion

B). Better penetration with less heat

C). Both less distortion and better penetration with less heat

D). None of these

Q 117. Which of the following is a reason of undercut in TIG welding

A). Unclean workpiece surface

B). Welding current too high

C). Insufficient shielding gas

D). All of these

Q 118. There is a standard colour indication for tungsten electrodes. Pure tungsten is marked

with______ colour

A). green

B). black

C). red

D). blue

Q 119. In straight polarity of TIG welding, ______% of the heat goes to the electrode end.

A). 30

B). 50

C). 70

D). 100

Q 120. Identify the welding joint shown in the figure.

A). Tee joint

B). Corner joint

C). Butt joint

D). Lap joint

Q 121. Which of the following is weld symbol for fillet joint

A). 30

B). 50

C). 70

D). 100

Q 122. Edge machining allowance in laser cutting is ________

A). 9.52 mm

B). 5.08 mm

C). 1.27 mm

D). 3.03 mm

Q 123. Which of the following is an advantage of plasma cutting

A). All metals and non-metals can be cut.

B). Cutting is possible in all positions.

C). Low cost of cutting

D). All of these

Q 124. Which of the following material cannot be cut with water jet cutting

A). Tempered glass

B). Plastic

C). Stone

D). Leather

INDUSTRIAL TRAINING INSTITUTE

Monthly Test-12, Marks- 20, Date:- ______________

(Every Question Carry Two Marks)

Q 1] Identify the welding joint shown in the picture]

A] Tee joint

B] Corner joint

C] Butt joint

D] Lap joint

Q 2] Combustion of oxy-acetylene flame produces about ________ degree

centigrade temperature]

A] 2400 to 2700

B] 1800 to 2200

C] 3100 to 3300

D] 1825 to 1875

Q 3] Acetylene gas is composed of carbon and ____________

A] argon
B] nitrogen
C] oxygen
D] Hydrogen
Q 4] The color of the acetylene gas cylinder is ______
A] green
B] black
C] maroon
D] Blue
Q 5] Which gas cylinder is also called as DA gas cylinder?
A] Acetylene gas cylinder
B] Oxygen gas cylinder
C] Argon gas cylinder
D] None of these
Q 6] 1 volume of liquid acetone can dissolve ________ volume of acetylene
gas under normal atmospheric pressure and temperature]
A] 10
B] 20
C] 25
D] 30
Q 7] Which one of the following is a type of gas regulator used in oxyacetylene
gas welding?
A] Single stage regulator
B] Double stage regulator
C] Both single and double stage regulator
D] None of these
Q 8] Identify the equipment shown in the picture]
A] Gas regulator
B] Welding blowpipe
C] Tip cleaner
D] Spark lighter
Q 9] In oxy acetylene gas cutting torch,the angle of the cutting nozzle
with the body is ___ degree]
A] 45
B] 60
C] 90

D] 120

Q 10] In oxy acetylene gas welding blowpipe, the angle of the welding nozzle with the neck is ____ degree]

A] 45

B] 60

C] 90

D] 120

www.ingramcontent.com/pod-product-compliance
Lightning Source LLC
LaVergne TN
LVHW010728090726
842905LV00040B/958